TO THE PARONTS

Dear Parents,

As your child's first and most important teacher, you can encourage your child's love of learning by participating in educational activities at home. Working together on the activities in this workbook will help your child build confidence, learn to reason, and develop skills necessary for early childhood education.

The following are some suggestions to help make your time together both enjoyable and rewarding.

- Choose a time when you and your child are relaxed.

- Provide a writing utensil that your child is familiar with.

- Don't attempt to do too many pages at one time or expect that every page be completed. Move on if your child is frustrated or loses interest.

- Praise your child's efforts.

- Discuss each page. Help your child relate the concepts in this book to everyday experiences.

ESSENTIAL SKILLS

The repetitive activities within each chapter have been designed to help children learn to sort, separate, put together, and figure out—the organizational skills so necessary for learning and thinking.

CHAPTER 1 Beginning Writing Skills
Learning to control the small muscles of the hand (**fine motor skill development**) allows the child to make the precise movements necessary for forming letters, while activities such as **writing from left to right, tracing,** and **forming lines** help to refine **eye/hand coordination.**

CHAPTER 2 Learning Letters
Children practice **tracing and writing letters** and recognizing which **upper and lower case letters** go together.

CHAPTER 3 Reading Readiness
Before learning to read, children must be able to visually distinguish same and different. For example, children usually recognize the difference between a cow and a horse before they recognize different letters. The emphasis in this chapter is on practicing various visual skills—**noticing details, making comparisons, matching figures, understanding directionality,** etc.

CHAPTER 4 Beginning Phonics
After practicing making **visual distinctions,** children can use **visual** and **auditory discrimination skills** to **recognize** and **reproduce initial and final consonant** sounds.

CHAPTER 5 Words That Rhyme
Children identify picture words and determine which words rhyme. **Word families** serve as an example of **rhyming words** that are spelled in a similar way.

CHAPTER 6 Colors and Shapes
Grouping things according to common attributes such as color, size, shape, etc. (**classification activities**), encourages development of a child's ability to reason and make **logical connections.**

CHAPTER 7 Math Readiness Skills
By **observing, reproducing, and continuing patterns,** children develop **visual memory** skills which prepare them for learning to recognize numbers. Various activities that focus on **making comparisons** also aid in the development of **number sense** and an understanding of mathematical order.

CHAPTER 8 Number Concepts
The emphasis in this chapter is on **identifying** and **creating sets of objects and their corresponding numerals,** and on **recognizing numerals** and **number words.** These activities prepare children for basic math—addition and subtraction—which is introduced in Modern Publishing's Grades K-1 companion to this book.

CHAPTER 9 Working With Numbers
Becoming familiar with the **order of numbers from 1-10, learning to write those numbers,** and **understanding the connection between a set of objects and its corresponding numeral,** all prepare a child to understand the concepts of addition and subtraction.

Jj

Follow the direction of each arrow. Then practice writing each letter.

J

j

Skills: Forming upper/lower case "j"; Writing left to right

K k

Follow the direction of each arrow. Then practice writing each letter.

Skills: Forming upper/lower case "k"; Writing left to right

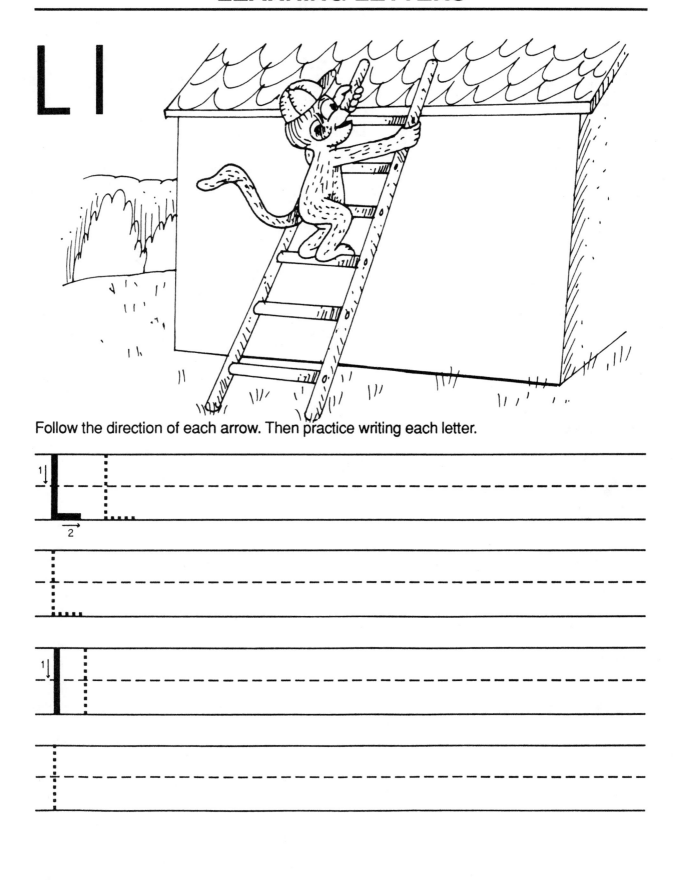

Follow the direction of each arrow. Then practice writing each letter.

Skills: Forming upper/lower case "l"; Writing left to right

Follow the direction of each arrow. Then practice writing each letter.

Skills: Forming upper/lower case "m"; Writing left to right

Follow the direction of each arrow. Then practice writing each letter.

Skills: Forming upper/lower case "n"; Writing left to right

LEARNING LETTERS

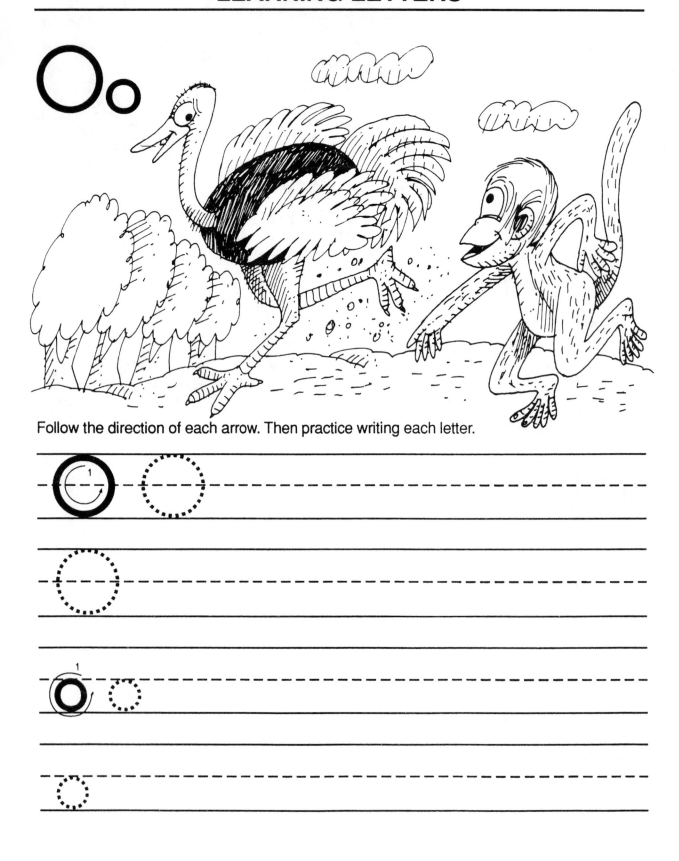

Follow the direction of each arrow. Then practice writing each letter.

Skills: Forming upper/lower case "o"; Writing left to right

Pp

Follow the direction of each arrow. Then practice writing each letter.

Skills: Forming upper/lower case "p"; Writing left to right

Follow the direction of each arrow. Then practice writing each letter.

Skills: Forming upper/lower case "q"; Writing left to right

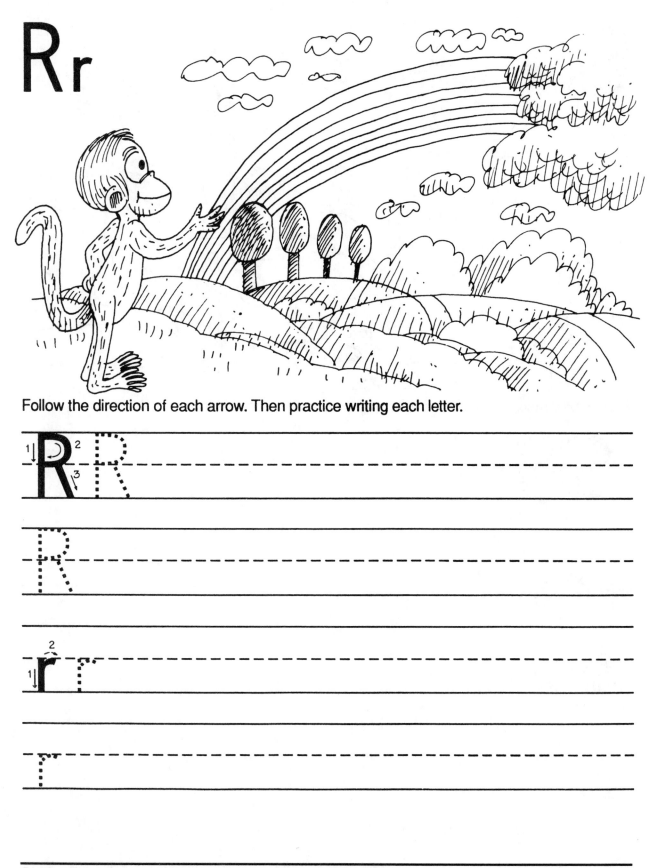

Follow the direction of each arrow. Then practice writing each letter.

Skills: Forming upper/lower case "r"; Writing left to right

Ss

Follow the direction of each arrow. Then practice writing each letter.

S S

s

s s

s

Skills: Forming upper/lower case "s"; Writing left to right

Follow the direction of each arrow. Then practice writing each letter.

Skills: Forming upper/lower case "v"; Writing left to right

Follow the direction of each arrow. Then practice writing each letter.

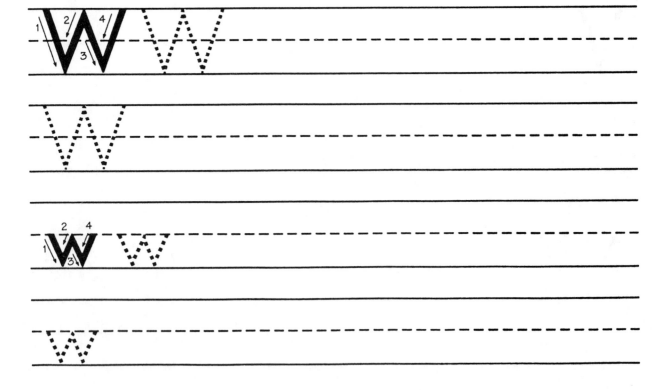

Skills: Forming upper/lower case "w"; Writing left to right

Follow the direction of each arrow. Then practice writing each letter.

Skills: Forming upper/lower case "x"; Writing left to right

Follow the direction of each arrow. Then practice writing each letter.

Skills: Forming upper/lower case "y"; Writing left to right

Z z

Follow the direction of each arrow. Then practice writing each letter.

Skills: Forming upper/lower case "z"; Writing left to right

LEARNING LETTERS

Trace each letter.

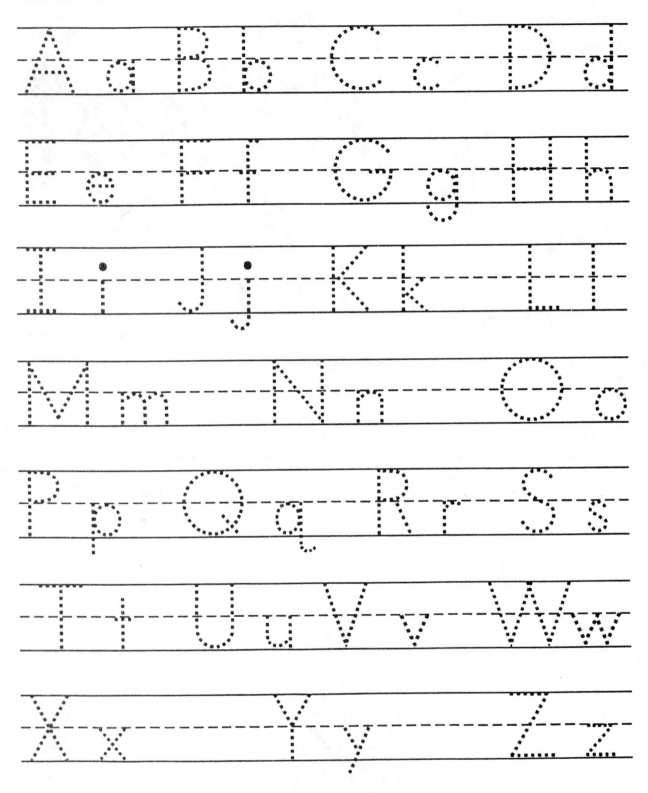

Skills: Forming upper/lower case letters; Writing the alphabet

READING READINESS

Look at the pictures in each row.
Circle the picture that goes in a different direction from the others.
Then color the pictures.

Skills: Visual discrimination; Understanding directionality; Following directions

READING READINESS

The fish at the top of the page is facing right.
Look at the rest of the pictures.
Circle the pictures that show fish facing right.

right

Skills: Recognizing directionality; Word recognition

READING READINESS

The snail at the top of the page is facing left.
Look at the rest of the pictures.
Circle the pictures that show snails facing left.

Skills: Recognizing directionality; Word recognition

READING READINESS

Look at the pictures at the top of this page.
One bird is facing right. One bird is facing left.
Then look at the rest of the pictures.
Circle the pictures that show animals facing right.
Draw a line under the pictures that show animals facing left.

Skills: Recognizing right and left; Word recognition

READING READINESS

Look at the pictures.
Draw a line between the pictures that are opposites.

Skills: Vocabulary; Opposites

READING READINESS

Look at the pictures.
Draw a line between the pictures that are opposites.

READING READINESS

Look at the socks on the clothesline.
Sort them into pairs by drawing a line between the matching socks.
Then color the page.

Skills: Understanding pairs; Visual matching

READING READINESS

Look at the mittens on this page.
Draw lines to match each pair.
Then color each pair a different color.

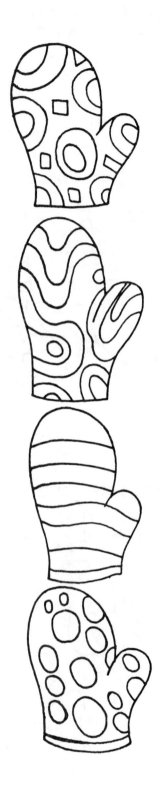

Skills: Understanding pairs; Visual matching

READING READINESS

Look at the pattern in each row.
Draw a line to the picture that continues each pattern.
Then color the pictures.

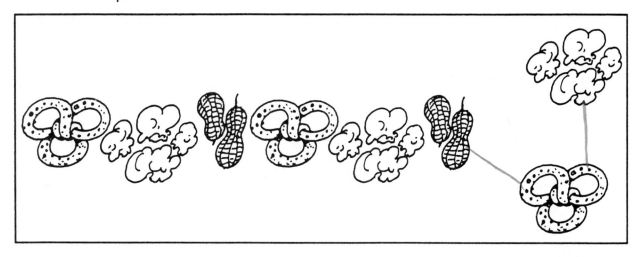

Skills: Observing and continuing patterns

READING READINESS

Look at the pattern in each row.
Draw the pictures that continue each pattern.
Then color the pictures.

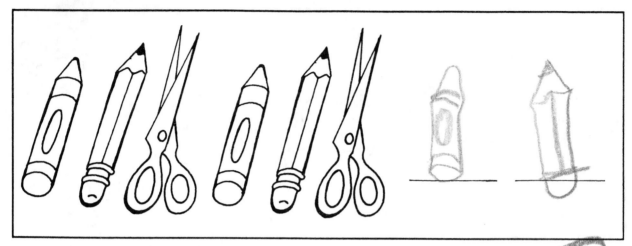

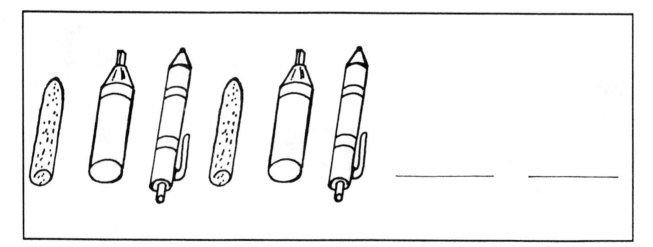

Skills: Observing and continuing patterns

READING READINESS

Look at the pattern in each row.
Draw the picture that continues each pattern.
Then color the pictures.

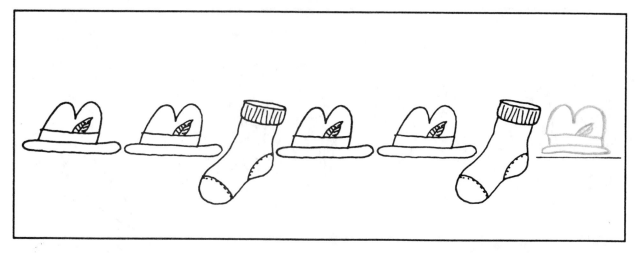

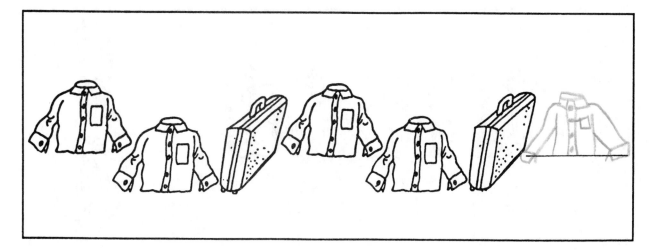

Skills: Observing and continuing patterns

READING READINESS

Look at the pattern in each row.
Draw a line to the picture that continues each pattern.
Then color the pictures.

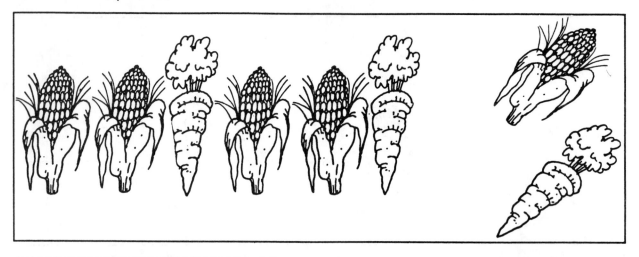

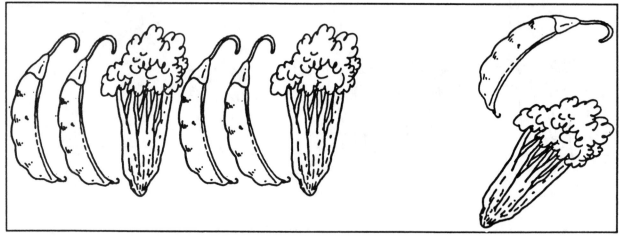

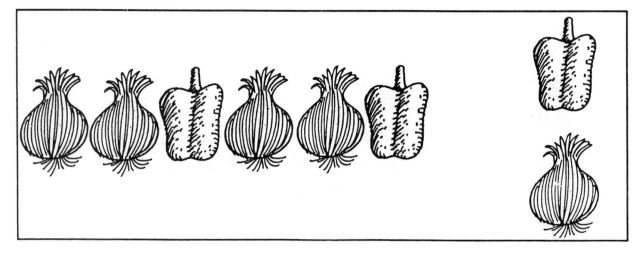

Skills: Observing and continuing patterns

Help the cat find her kittens.

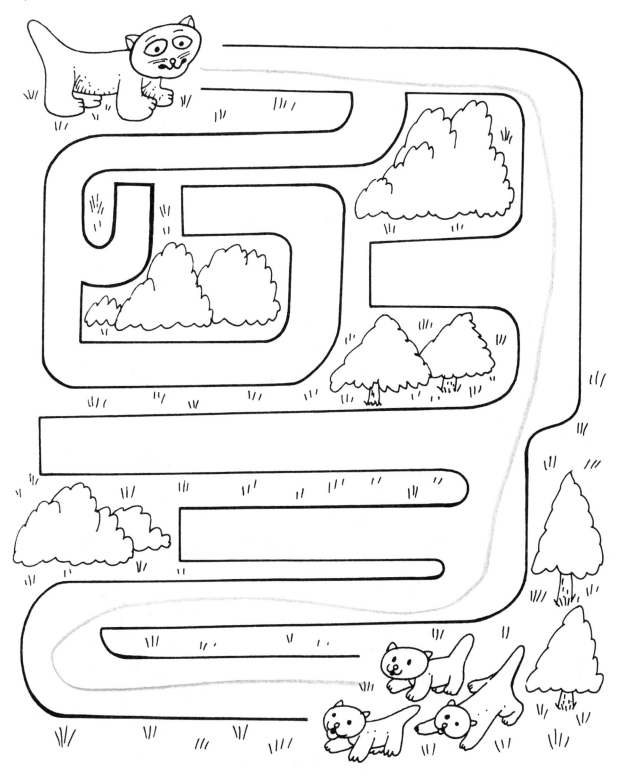

Skills: Visual perception; Fine motor skill development

READING READINESS

Help these children find their way to school.

Skills: Visual perception; Fine motor skill development

Here are some foods you might like to eat.
Look carefully at each food.
When you are ready, turn the page to play a memory game.

Skills: Visual memory; Association; Following directions

READING READINESS

Look at the pictures on this page.
Which ones do you remember from the last page?
Circle the ones you remember. Then color all the pictures.

Skills: Visual memory; Association; Following directions

The "d" sound

Dd

Which ones begin with d? Color them red.

Skills: Recognition of the "d" sound; Sound/symbol association

BEGINNING PHONICS

The "l" sound

Ll

Which ones begin with l? Color them yellow.

Skills: Recognition of the "l" sound; Sound/symbol association

BEGINNING PHONICS

The "z" sound

Zz

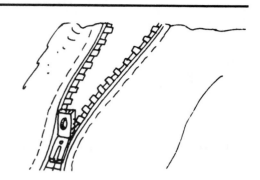

Which ones begin with z? Color them green.

Skills: Recognition of the "z" sound; Sound/symbol association

BEGINNING PHONICS

The "n" sound

Nn

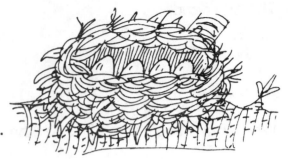

Which ones begin with n? Color them brown.

Skills: Recognition of the "n" sound; Sound/symbol association

The "q" sound

Qq

Which ones begin with q? Color them blue.

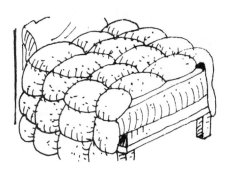

Skills: Recognition of the "q" sound; Sound/symbol association

BEGINNING PHONICS

The "r" sound

Rr

Which ones begin with r? Color them red.

Skills: Recognition of the "r" sound; Sound/symbol association

BEGINNING PHONICS

The "s" sound

Ss

Which ones begin with s? Color them yellow.

Skills: Recognition of the "s" sound; Sound/symbol association

BEGINNING PHONICS

The "t" sound

Tt

Which ones begin with t? Color them orange.

Skills: Recognition of the "t" sound; Sound/symbol association

BEGINNING PHONICS

The "b" sound

Bb

Which ones begin with b? Say each "b" word out loud.

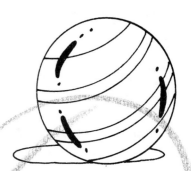

Skills: Auditory discrimination; Recognition of the "b" sound; Sound/symbol association

BEGINNING PHONICS

The "f" sound

Ff

Which ones begin with f? Say each "f" word out loud.

Skills: Auditory discrimination; Recognition of the "f" sound; Sound/symbol association

BEGINNING PHONICS

The "g" sound

Gg

Which ones begin with g? Say each "g" word out loud.

Skills: Auditory discrimination; Recognition of the "g" sound; Sound/symbol association

BEGINNING PHONICS

The "k" sound

Kk

Which ones begin with k? Say each "k" word out loud.

Skills: Auditory discrimination; Recognition of the "k" sound; Sound/symbol association

BEGINNING PHONICS

The "v" sound

V v

Which ones begin with v? Say each "v" word out loud.

Skills: Auditory discrimination; Recognition of the "v" sound; Sound/symbol association

BEGINNING PHONICS

The "c" sound

Cc

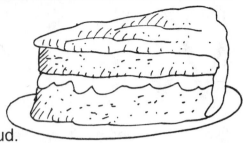

Which ones begin with c? Say each "c" word out loud.

Skills: Auditory discrimination; Recognition of the "c" sound; Sound/symbol association

The "h" sound

Hh

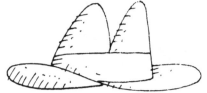

Which ones begin with h? Say each "h" word out loud.

Skills: Auditory discrimination; Recognition of the "h" sound; Sound/symbol association

BEGINNING PHONICS

The "m" sound

Mm

Which ones begin with m? Say each "m" word out loud.

Skills: Auditory discrimination; Recognition of the "m" sound; Sound/symbol association

BEGINNING PHONICS

The "p" sound

Pp

Which ones begin with p? Say each "p" word out loud.

Skills: Auditory discrimination; Recognition of the "p" sound; Sound/symbol association

BEGINNING PHONICS

The "y" sound

Y y

Which ones begin with y? Say each "y" word out loud.

Skills: Auditory discrimination; Recognition of the "y" sound; Sound/symbol association

BEGINNING PHONICS

The "d" sound

Dd

Which ones begin with d? Say each "d" word out loud.

Skills: Auditory discrimination; Recognition of the "d" sound; Sound/symbol association

The "j" sound

Jj

Which ones begin with j? Say each "j" word out loud.

Skills: Auditory discrimination; Recognition of the "j" sound; Sound/symbol association

BEGINNING PHONICS

The "l" sound

Ll

Which ones begin with l? Say each "l" word out loud.

Skills: Auditory discrimination; Recognition of the "l" sound; Sound/symbol association

BEGINNING PHONICS

The "w" sound

Ww

Which ones begin with w? Say each "w" word out loud.

Skills: Auditory discrimination; Recognition of the "w" sound; Sound/symbol association

BEGINNING PHONICS

The "z" sound

Zz

Which ones begin with z? Say each "z" word out loud.

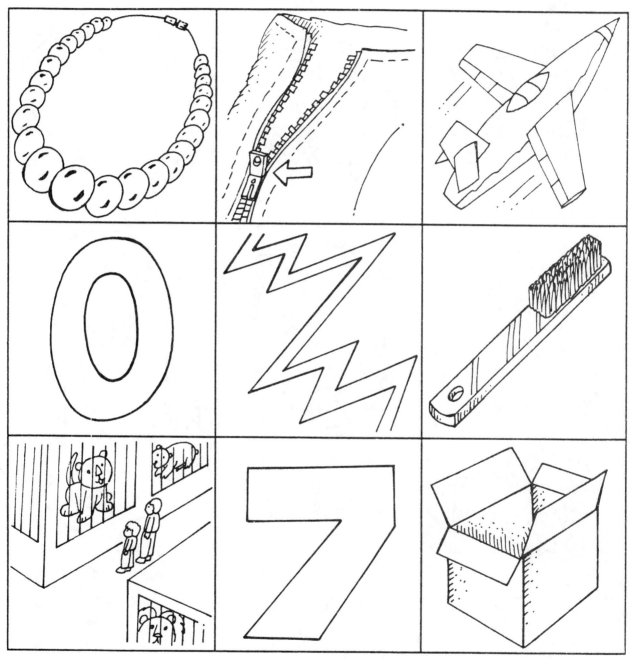

Skills: Auditory discrimination; Recognition of the "z" sound; Sound/symbol association

BEGINNING PHONICS

The "n" sound

Nn

Which ones begin with n? Say each "n" word out loud.

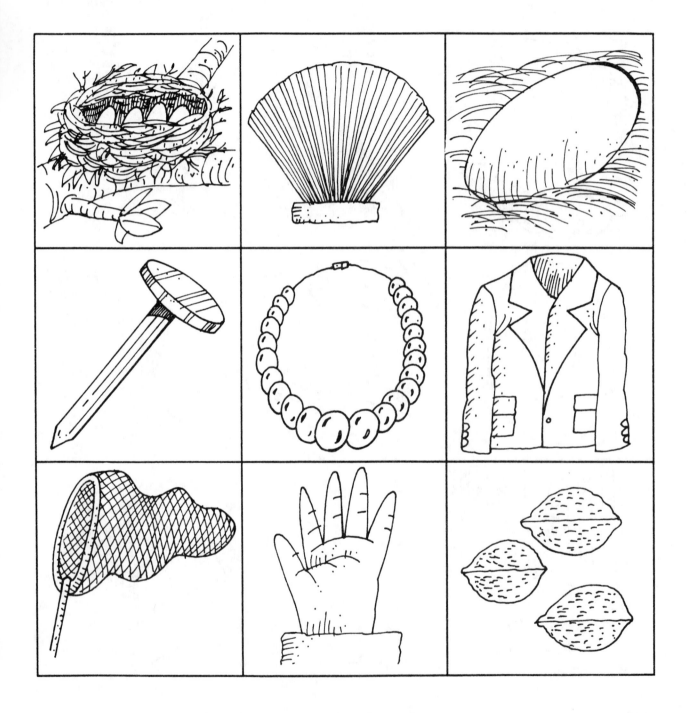

Skills: Auditory discrimination; Recognition of the "n" sound; Sound/symbol association

BEGINNING PHONICS

The "q" sound

Qq

Which ones begin with q? Say each "q" word out loud.

Skills: Auditory discrimination; Recognition of the "q" sound; Sound/symbol association

BEGINNING PHONICS

The "r" sound

Rr

Which ones begin with r? Say each "r" word out loud.

Skills: Auditory discrimination; Recognition of the "r" sound; Sound/symbol association

BEGINNING PHONICS

The "s" sound

Ss

Which ones begin with s? Say each "s" word out loud.

Skills: Auditory discrimination; Recognition of the "s" sound; Sound/symbol association

BEGINNING PHONICS

The "t" sound

T t

Which ones begin with t? Say each "t" word out loud.

Skills: Auditory discrimination; Recognition of the "t" sound; Sound/symbol association

BEGINNING PHONICS

Say the name of each picture. Listen to the first sound.
Then circle the letters with that sound.

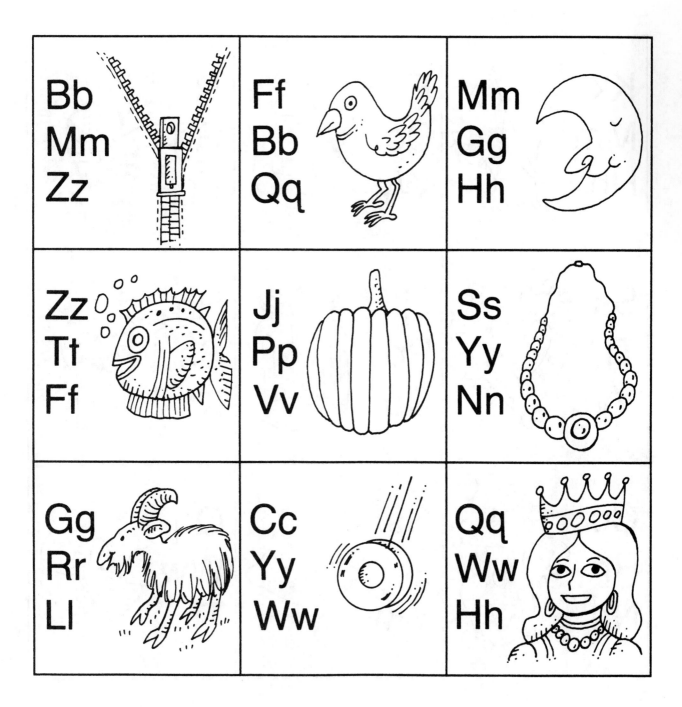

BEGINNING PHONICS

Say the name of each picture. Listen to the first sound.
Then circle the letters with that sound.

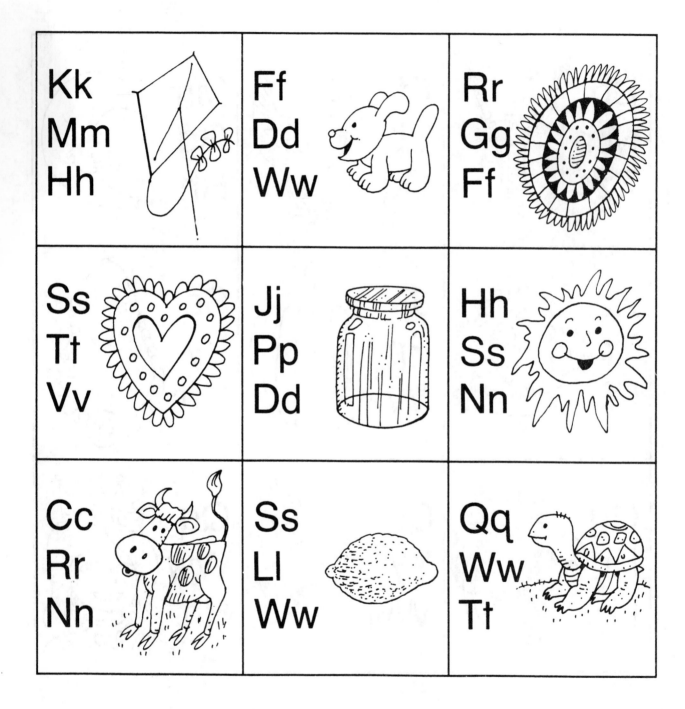

Kk Mm Hh	Ff Dd Ww	Rr Gg Ff
Ss Tt Vv	Jj Pp Dd	Hh Ss Nn
Cc Rr Nn	Ss Ll Ww	Qq Ww Tt

Skills: Auditory and visual discrimination; Recognition of sounds and their symbols

BEGINNING PHONICS

Say the name of each picture. Listen to the first sound.
Then circle the letters with that sound.

Hh Mm Kk	Ff Bb Ss	Ww Gg Hh
Rr Nn Cc	Ll Pp Hh	Ss Mm Nn
Kk Rr Ll	Dd Yy Vv	Bb Ww Ff

Skills: Auditory and visual discrimination; Recognition of sounds and their symbols

BEGINNING PHONICS

Look at the letters in each row.
Circle the picture whose name begins with that sound.

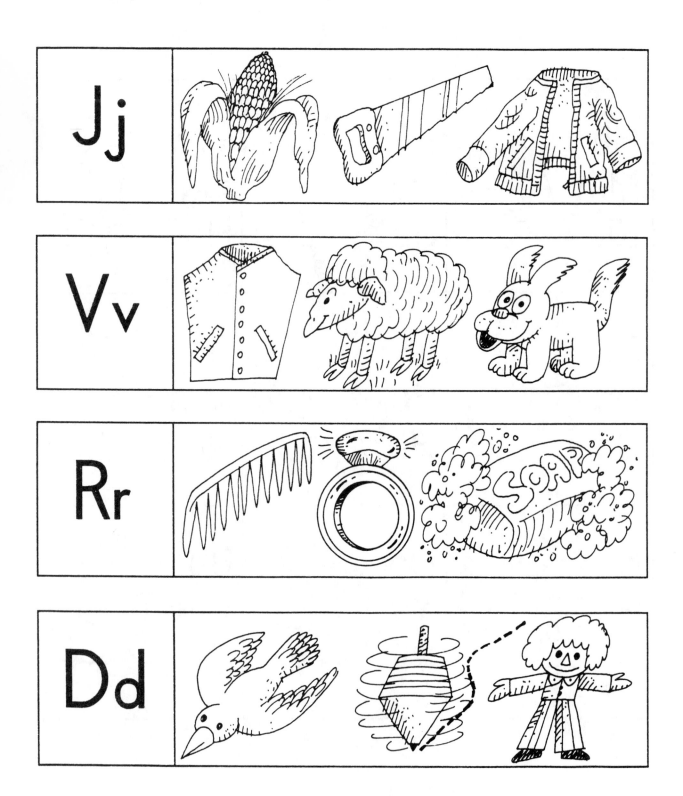

BEGINNING PHONICS

Look at the letters in each row.
Circle the **picture** whose name begins with that sound.

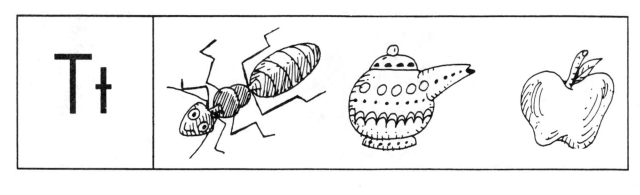

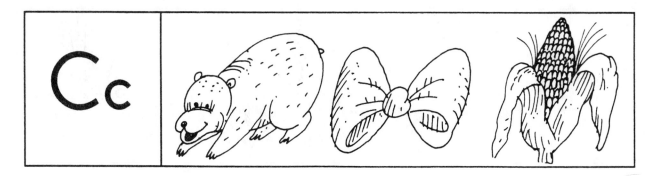

Skills: Recognition of sounds and their symbols

BEGINNING PHONICS

Look at the letters in each row.
Circle the picture whose name begins with that sound.

Zz

Mm

Pp

Ff

Skills: Recognition of sounds and their symbols

BEGINNING PHONICS

Look at the letters in each row.
Circle the picture whose name begins with that sound.

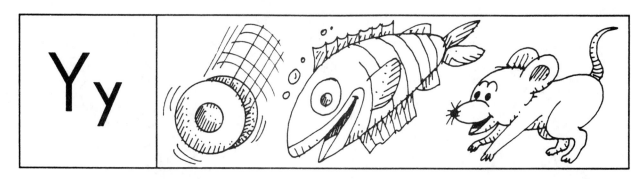

Skills: Recognition of sounds and their symbols

BEGINNING PHONICS

Say the name of each picture.
Draw a line from each letter to the picture whose name ends with that sound.

b   g   m   d   t

Skills: Recognition of sounds and their symbols

BEGINNING PHONICS

Look at the letter in each row.
Circle the picture whose name ends with that sound.

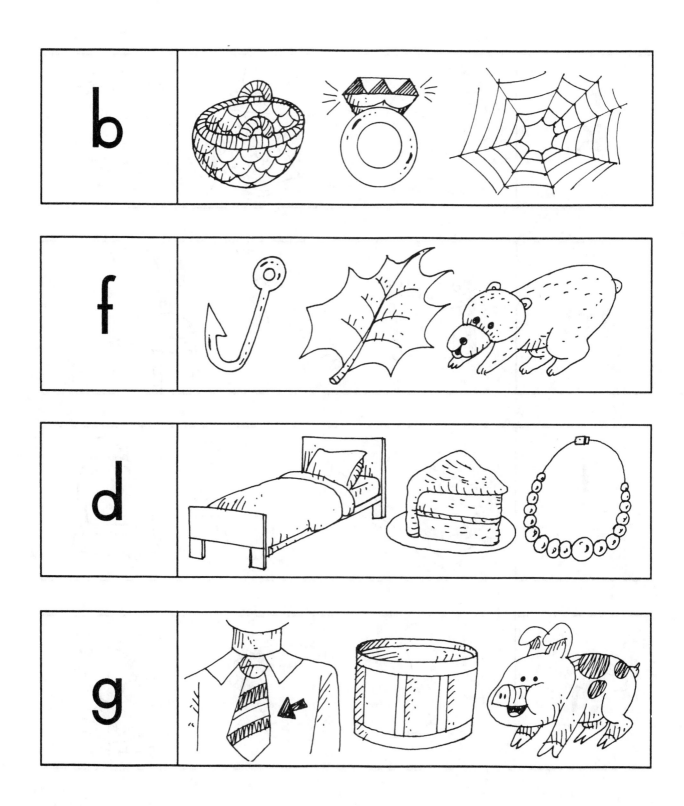

BEGINNING PHONICS

Look at the letter in each row.
Circle the picture whose name ends with that sound.

BEGINNING PHONICS

Look at the letter in each row.
Circle the picture whose name ends with that sound.

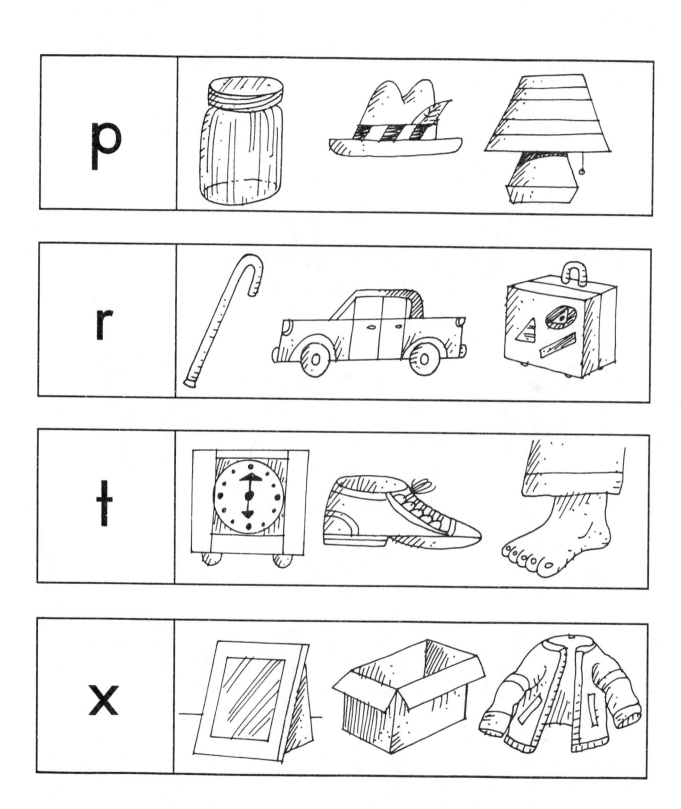

Skills: Recognition of sounds and their symbols

BEGINNING PHONICS

Final consonant: b

crib

Say the name of each picture.
Draw a line from the letter b
   to each picture whose name
   ends with the "b" sound.

Skills: Recognition of the final consonant "b" sound; Sound/symbol association

Final consonant: f

leaf

Say the name of each picture.
Draw a line from the letter f
  to each picture whose name
  ends with the "f" sound.

Skills: Recognition of the final consonant "f" sound; Sound/symbol association

Final consonant: d

sled

Say the name of each picture.
Draw a line from the letter d
to each picture whose name
ends with the "d" sound.

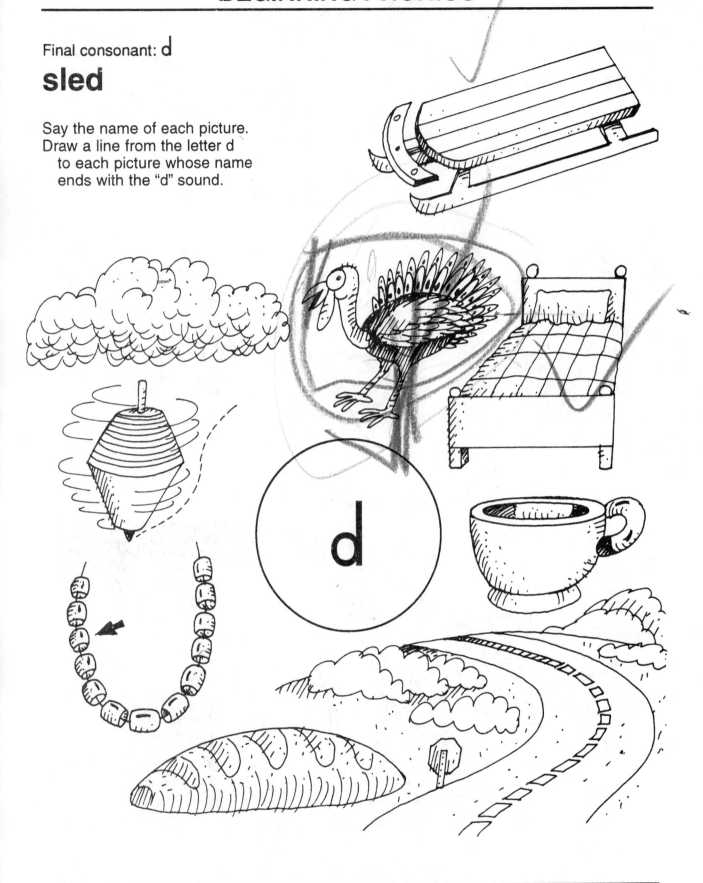

BEGINNING PHONICS

Final consonant: g

bag

Say the name of each picture.
Draw a line from the letter g
to each picture whose name
ends with the "g" sound.

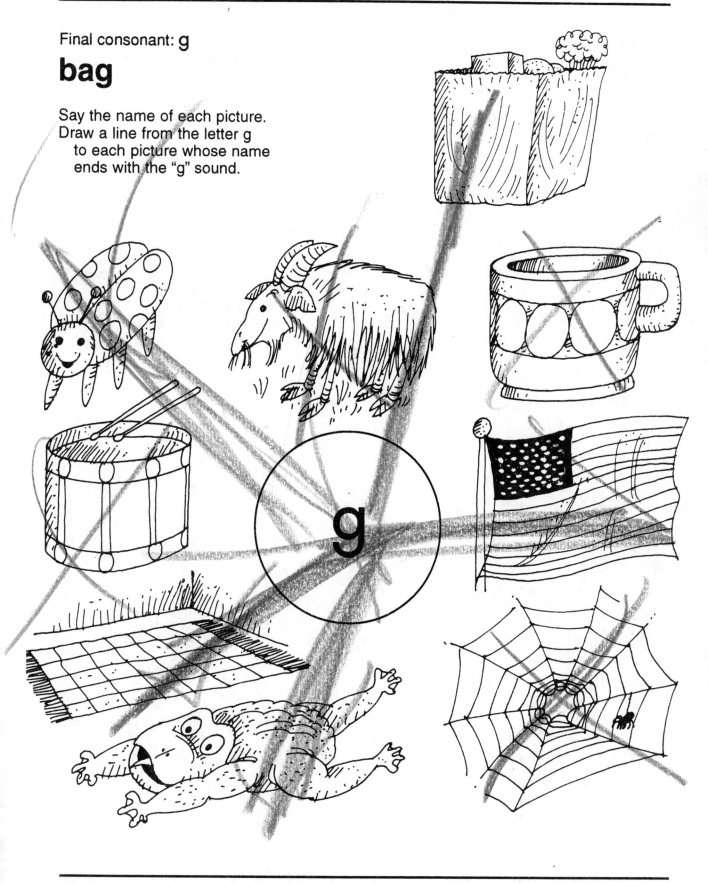

Skills: Recognition of the final consonant "g" sound; Sound/symbol association

Final consonant: k

hook

Say the name of each picture.
Draw a line from the letter k
    to each picture whose name
    ends with the "k" sound.

Skills: Recognition of the final consonant "k" sound; Sound/symbol association

Final consonant: m

broom

Say the name of each picture.
Draw a line from the letter m
   to each picture whose name
   ends with the "m" sound.

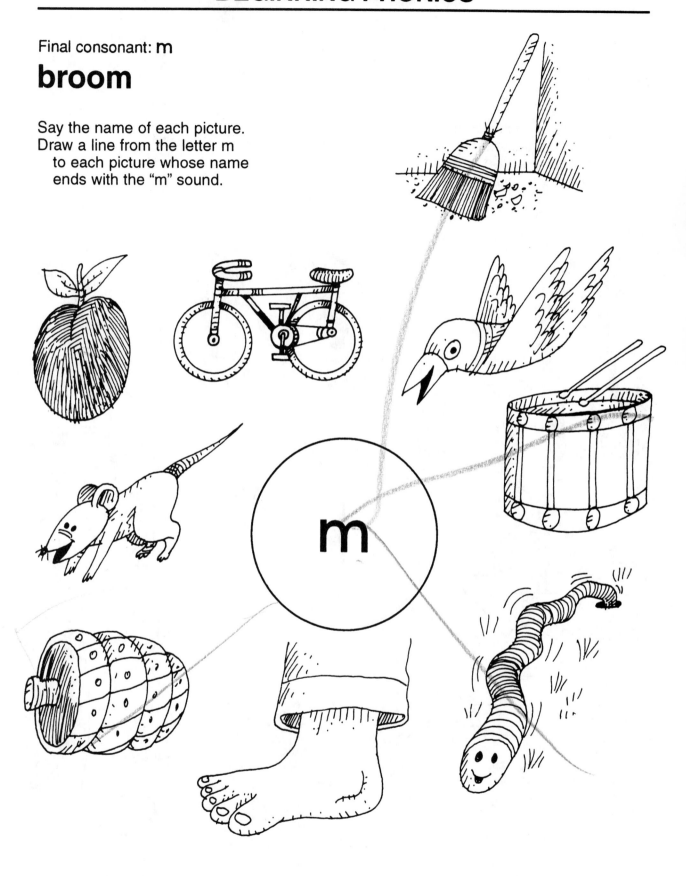

Skills: Recognition of the final consonant "m" sound; Sound/symbol association

BEGINNING PHONICS

Final consonant: l

sail

Say the name of each picture.
Draw a line from the letter l
   to each picture whose name
   ends with the "l" sound.

Skills: Recognition of the final consonant "l" sound; Sound/symbol association

Final consonant: **n**

chain

Say the name of each picture.
Draw a line from the letter n
  to each picture whose name
  ends with the "n" sound.

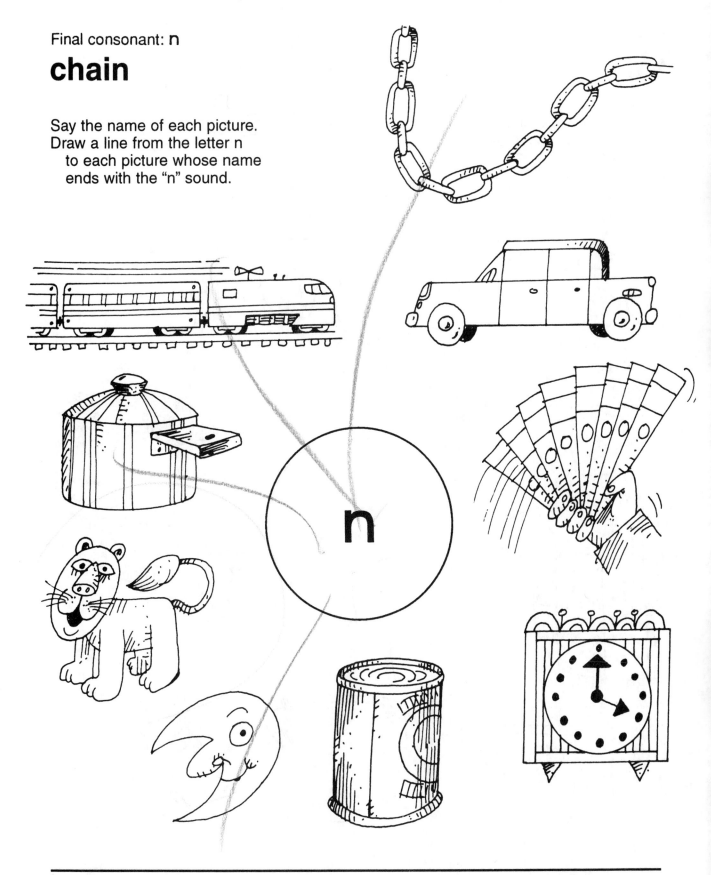

Skills: Recognition of the final consonant "n" sound; Sound/symbol association

BEGINNING PHONICS

Final consonant: p

top

Say the name of each picture.
Draw a line from the letter p
to each picture whose name
ends with the "p" sound.

Skills: Recognition of the final consonant "p" sound; Sound/symbol association

Final consonant: **r**

deer

Say the name of each picture.
Draw a line from the letter r
  to each picture whose name
  ends with the "r" sound.

Skills: Recognition of the final consonant "r" sound; Sound/symbol association

BEGINNING PHONICS

Final consonant: t

cat

Say the name of each picture.
Draw a line from the letter t
to each picture whose name
ends with the "t" sound.

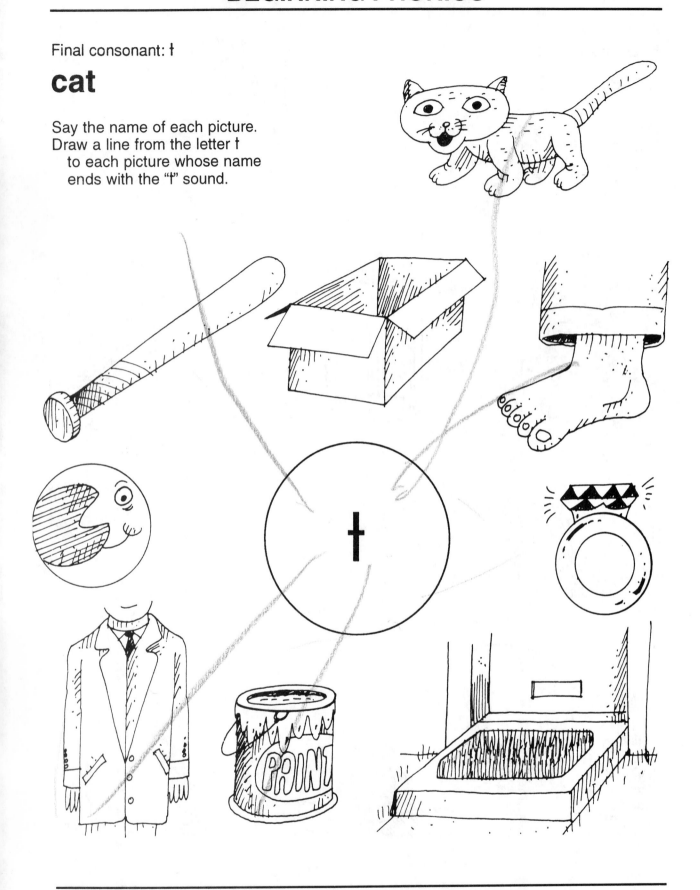

Skills: Recognition of the final consonant "t" sound; Sound/symbol association

BEGINNING PHONICS

Final consonant: X

six

Say the name of each picture.
Draw a line from the letter x
   to each picture whose name
   ends with the "x" sound.

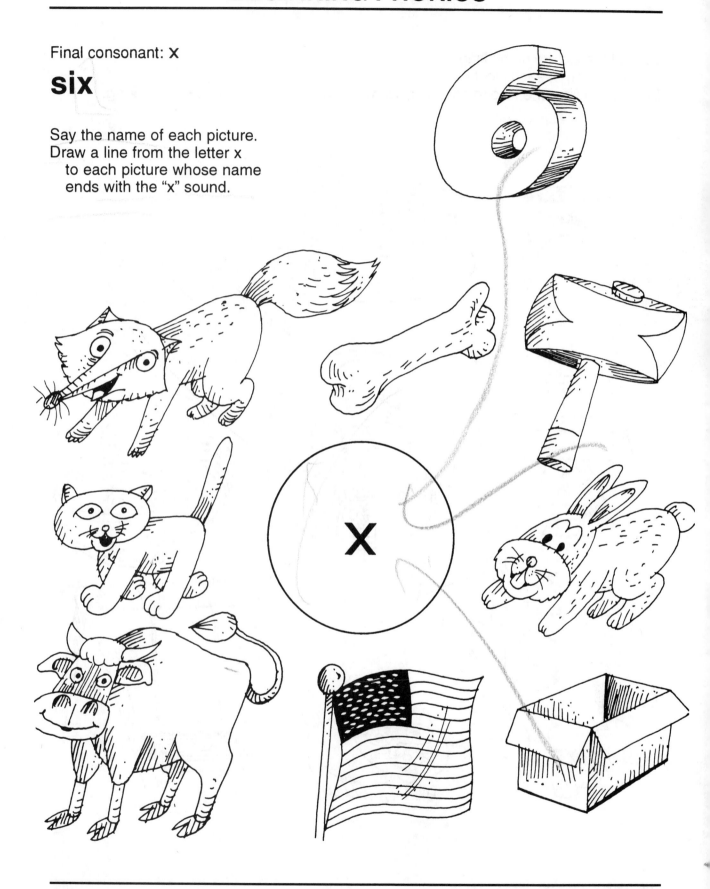

Skills: Recognition of the final consonant "x" sound; Sound/symbol association

WORDS THAT RHYME

Look at the picture of the king.
Say the name of each picture.
Draw a line from the king to each picture whose name rhymes with the word **king**.

Skills: Recognizing rhyming words

WORDS THAT RHYME

Look at the picture of the cat.
Say the name of each picture.
Craw a line from the cat to each picture whose name rhymes with the word **cat**.

Skills: Recognizing rhyming words

WORDS THAT RHYME

Look at the picture of the bear.
Say the name of each picture.
Draw a line from the bear to each picture whose name rhymes with the word **bear**.

WORDS THAT RHYME

Look at the picture of the bug.
Say the name of each picture.
Draw a line from the bug to each picture whose name rhymes with the word **bug**.

Skills: Recognizing rhyming words

WORDS THAT RHYME

Look at the picture of the train.
Say the name of each picture.
Draw a line from the train to each picture whose name rhymes with the word **train**.

Skills: Recognizing rhyming words

WORDS THAT RHYME

Look at the picture of the hen.
Say the name of each picture.
Draw a line from the hen to each picture whose name rhymes with the word **hen**.

Skills: Recognizing rhyming words

WORDS THAT RHYME

Look at the first picture in each row and say its name.
Circle the picture whose name rhymes with it.

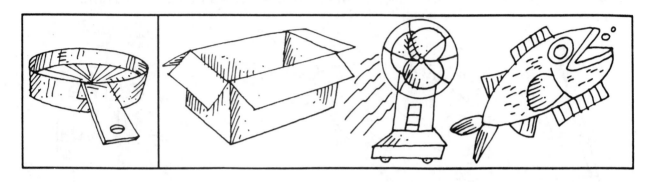

Skills: Recognizing rhyming words

WORDS THAT RHYME

Look at the first picture in each row and say its name.
Circle the picture whose name rhymes with it.

WORDS THAT RHYME

Look at the first picture in each row and say its name.
Circle the picture whose name rhymes with it.

WORDS THAT RHYME

Look at the first picture in each row and say its name.
Circle the picture whose name rhymes with it.

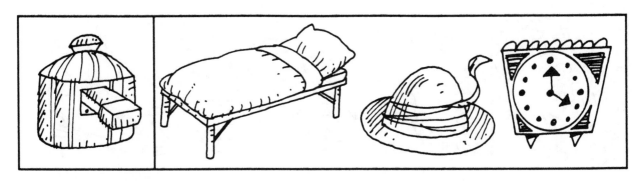

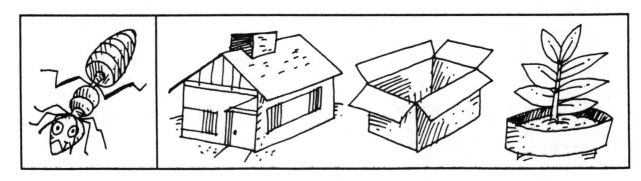

Skills: Recognizing rhyming words

WORDS THAT RHYME

Look at the first picture in each row and say its name.
Circle the picture whose name rhymes with it.

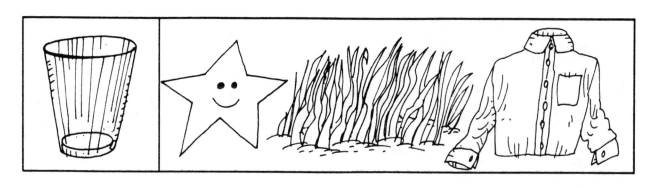

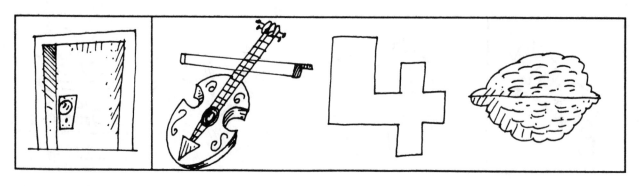

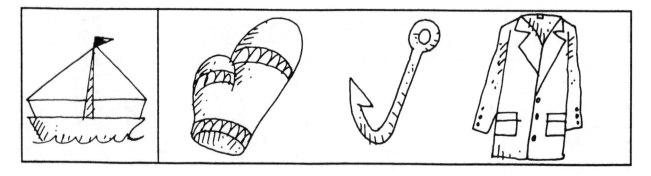

Skills: Recognizing rhyming words

WORDS THAT RHYME

Look at the first picture in each row and say its name.
Circle the picture whose name rhymes with it.

Skills: Recognizing rhyming words

WORDS THAT RHYME

Look at each picture and say its name.
Draw a line to match each rhyming picture.

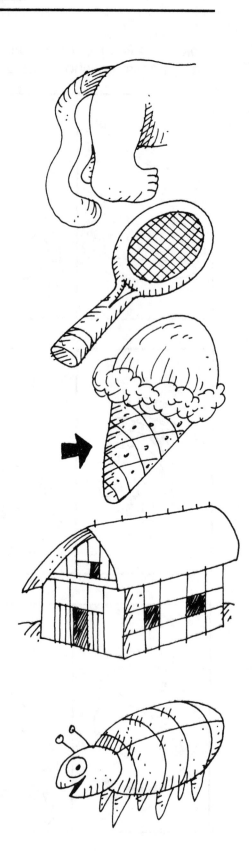

WORDS THAT RHYME

Look at each picture and say its name.
Draw a line to match each rhyming picture.

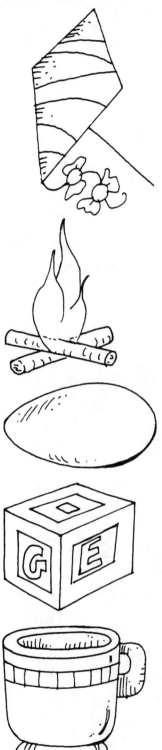

Skills: Recognizing rhyming words

WORDS THAT RHYME

Look at each picture and say its name.
Draw a line to match each rhyming picture.

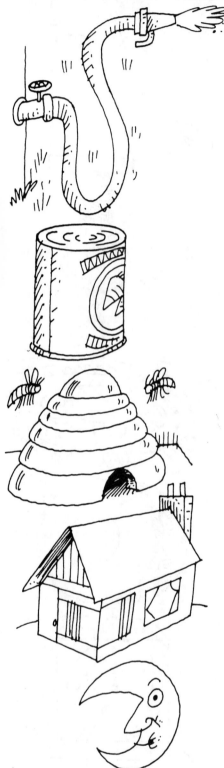

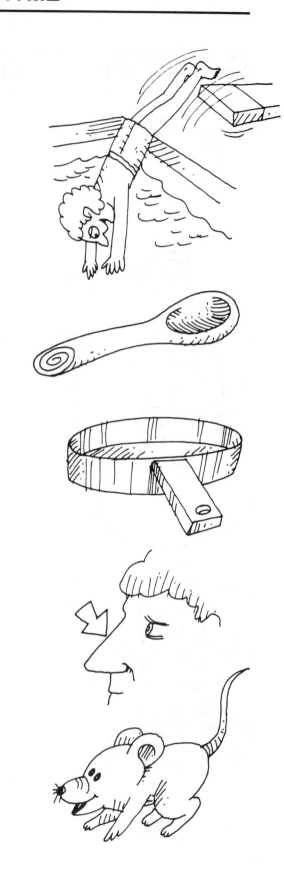

Skills: Recognizing rhyming words

WORDS THAT RHYME

Look at each picture and say its name.
Draw a line to match each rhyming picture.

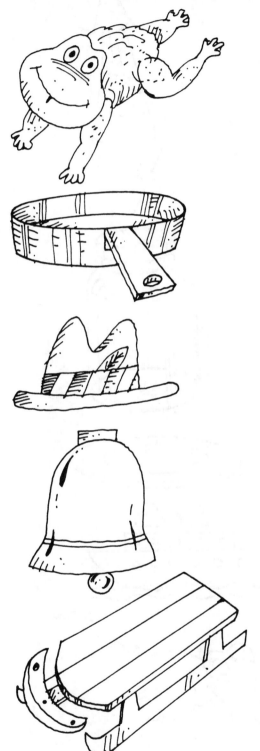

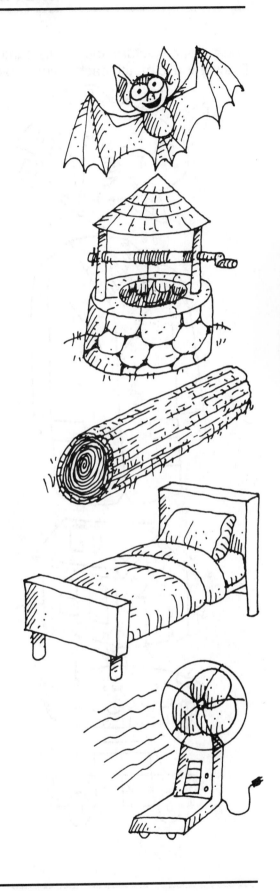

WORDS THAT RHYME

Look at each picture and say its name.
Draw a line to match each rhyming picture.

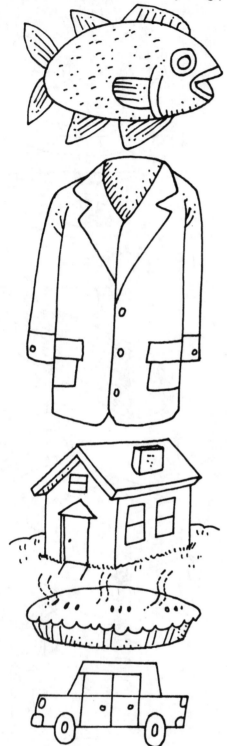

WORDS THAT RHYME

Look at each picture and say its name.
Draw a line to match each rhyming picture.

WORDS THAT RHYME

Look at each picture and say its name.
Draw a line to match each rhyming picture.

Skills: Recognizing rhyming words

WORDS THAT RHYME

The word **bat** is part of the **at** family.
Name these other things in the **at** family.

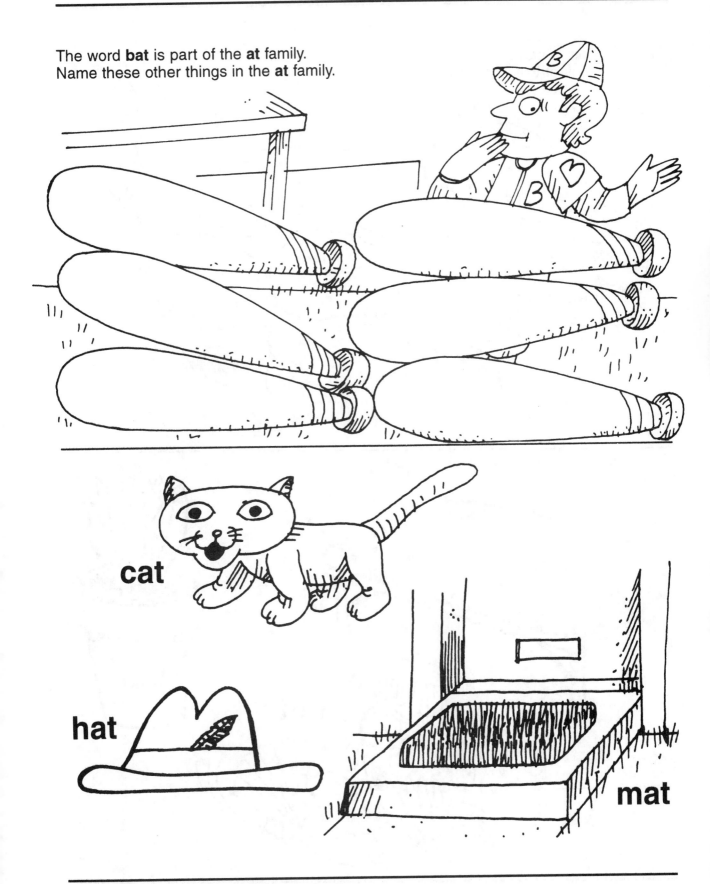

cat

hat

mat

Skills: Recognizing words in the **at** family

WORDS THAT RHYME

The word **spot** is part of the **ot** family.
Name these other things in the **ot** family.

cot

pot

hot

Skills: Recognizing words in the **ot** family

WORDS THAT RHYME

The word **cake** is part of the **ake** family.
Name these other things in the **ake** family.

snake

rake

lake

Skills: Recognizing words in the **ake** family

WORDS THAT RHYME

The word **bug** is part of the **ug** family.
Name these other things in the **ug** family.

mug

jug

rug

Skills: Recognizing words in the **ug** family

WORDS THAT RHYME

The word **swing** is part of the **ing** family.
Name these other things in the **ing** family.

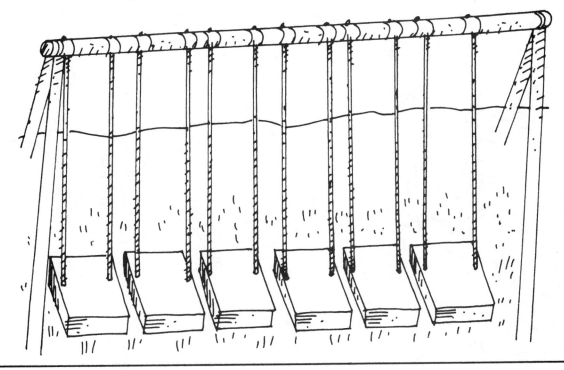

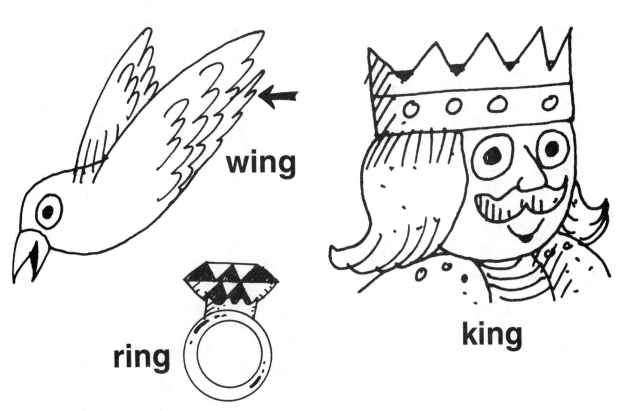

wing

ring

king

Skills: Recognizing words in the **ing** family

WORDS THAT RHYME

The word **clown** is part of the **own** family.
Name these other things in the **own** family.

crown

frown

down

Skills: Recognizing words in the **own** family

red

Color these things that are red.

Skills: Distinguishing color; Classification; Word recognition

yellow

Color these things that are yellow.

blue

Color these things that are blue.

Skills: Distinguishing color; Classification; Word recognition

orange

Color these things that are orange.

Skills: Distinguishing color; Classification; Word recognition

purple

Color these things that are purple.

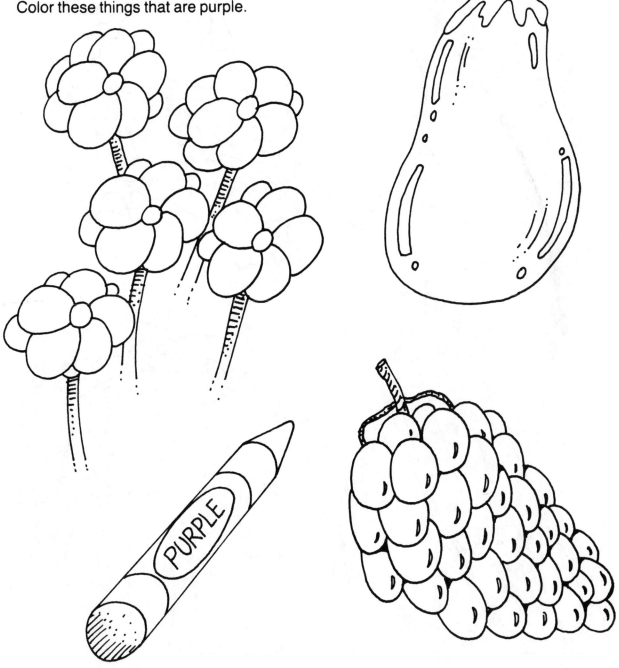

Skills: Distinguishing color; Classification; Word recognition

green

Color these things that are green.

Skills: Distinguishing color; Classification; Word recognition

black

Color these things that are black.

Skills: Distinguishing color; Classification; Word recognition

brown

Color these things that are brown.

Skills: Distinguishing color; Classification; Word recognition

COLORS AND SHAPES

Look at the balloons.
Color each balloon to match the color word.
Then color
the picture.

Skills: Distinguishing color; Visual memory of sight vocabulary

COLORS AND SHAPES

Look at the fish swimming in the ocean.
Color them to match the color words.
Then color the ocean blue.

Skills: Distinguishing color; Visual memory of sight vocabulary

COLORS AND SHAPES

Color each picture to match the color word.
Then look at the color word in each box.
Draw something that is that color.

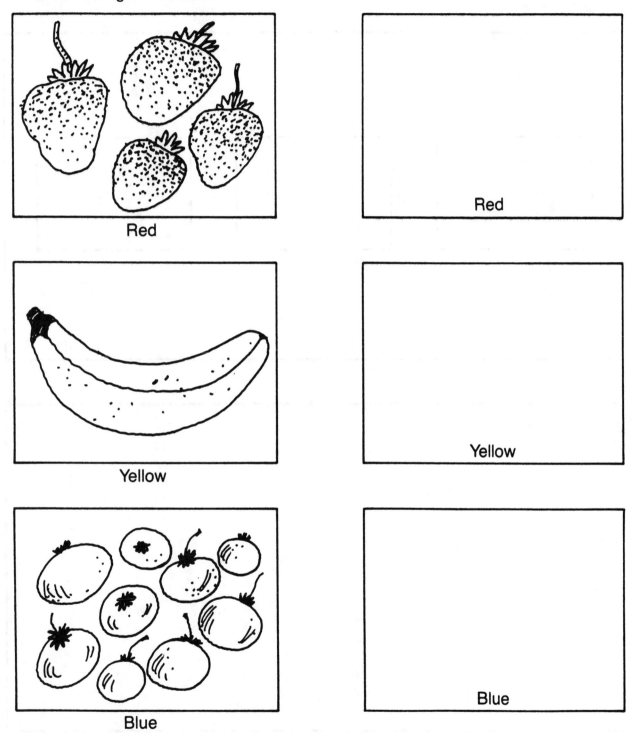

Red

Red

Yellow

Yellow

Blue

Blue

Skills: Following directions; Matching colors to color words; Responding creatively

COLORS AND SHAPES

Trace the rectangles.
Then draw your own rectangles.
Color the shapes.

Skills: Fine motor skill development; Shape recognition

COLORS AND SHAPES

Look at the rectangles at the top of the page.
Circle the objects that are shaped like rectangles.

COLORS AND SHAPES

Trace the squares.
Then draw your own squares.
Color the shapes.

COLORS AND SHAPES

Look at the squares at the top of the page.
Circle the objects that are shaped like squares.

Skills: Shape recognition; Visual discrimination; Recognizing shapes in objects

COLORS AND SHAPES

Trace the triangles.
Then draw your own triangles.
Color the shapes.

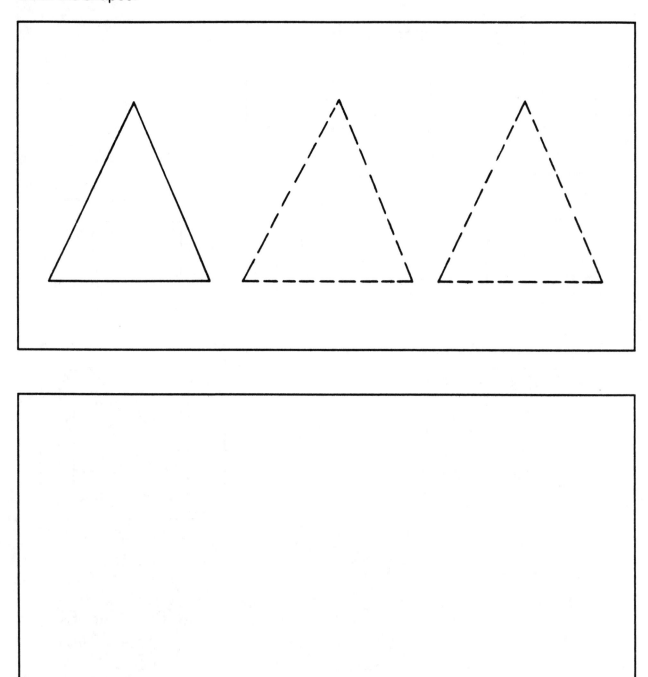

Skills: Fine motor skill development; Shape recognition

COLORS AND SHAPES

Look at the triangles at the top of the page.
Circle the objects that are shaped like triangles.

Skills: Shape recognition; Visual discrimination; Recognizing shapes in objects

COLORS AND SHAPES

Trace the circles.
Then draw your own circles.
Color the shapes.

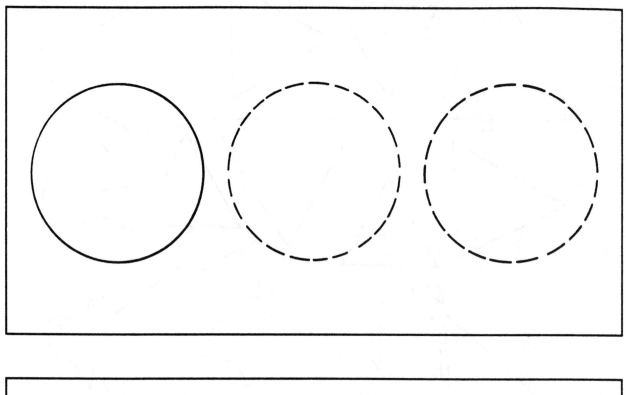

Skills: Fine motor skill development; Shape recognition

COLORS AND SHAPES

Look at the circles at the top of the page.
Circle the objects that are shaped like circles.

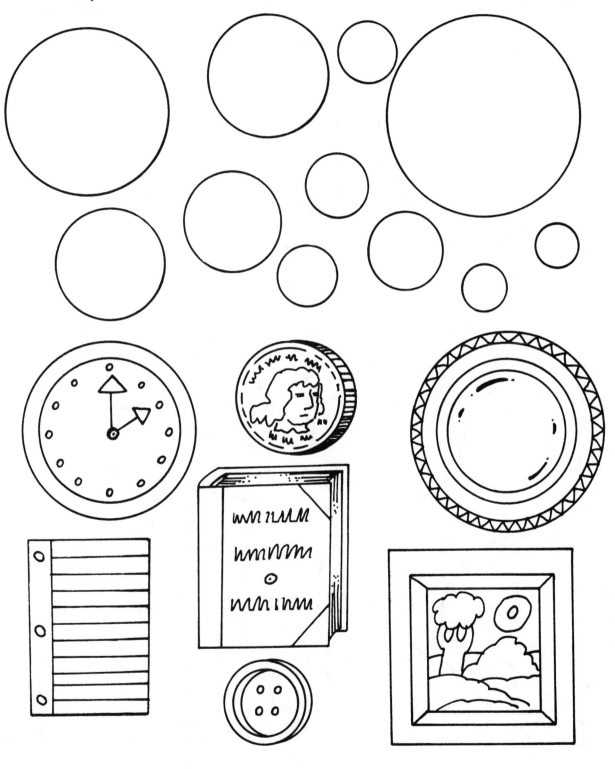

Skills: Shape recognition; Visual discrimination; Recognizing shapes in objects

COLORS AND SHAPES

Look at the circle. Look at the rectangle.
Color the circles yellow.
Color the rectangles green.

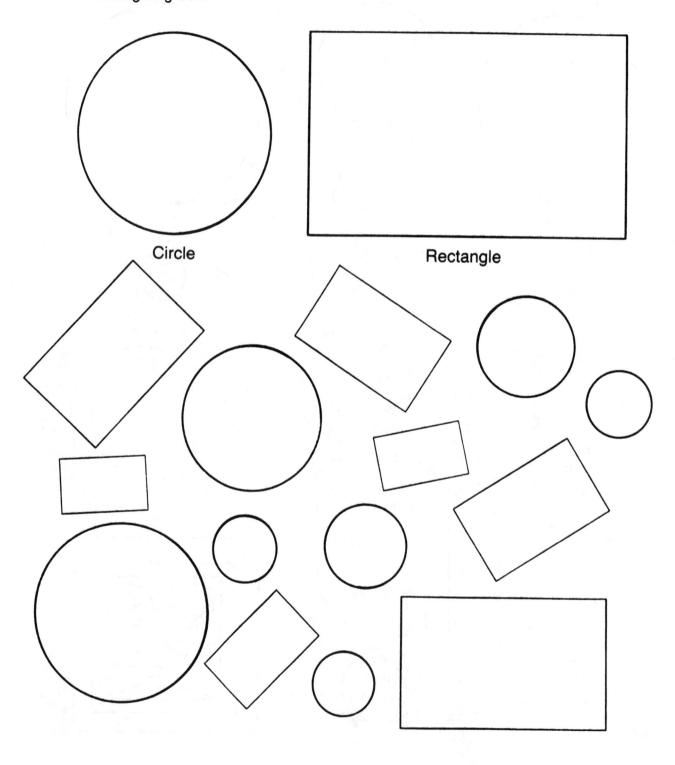

Circle   Rectangle

COLORS AND SHAPES

Look at the triangle. Look at the square.
Color the triangles red.
Color the squares blue.

Triangle Square

Skills: Shape recognition; Visual discrimination

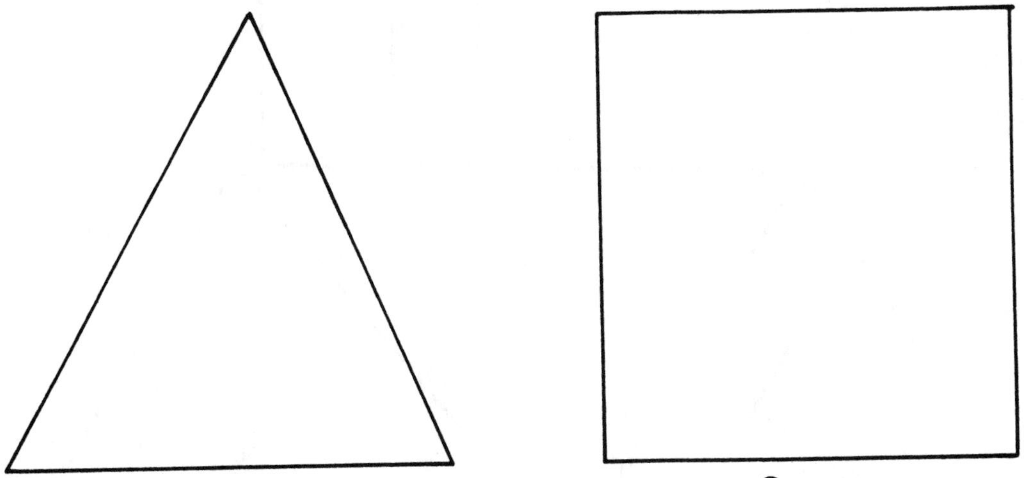

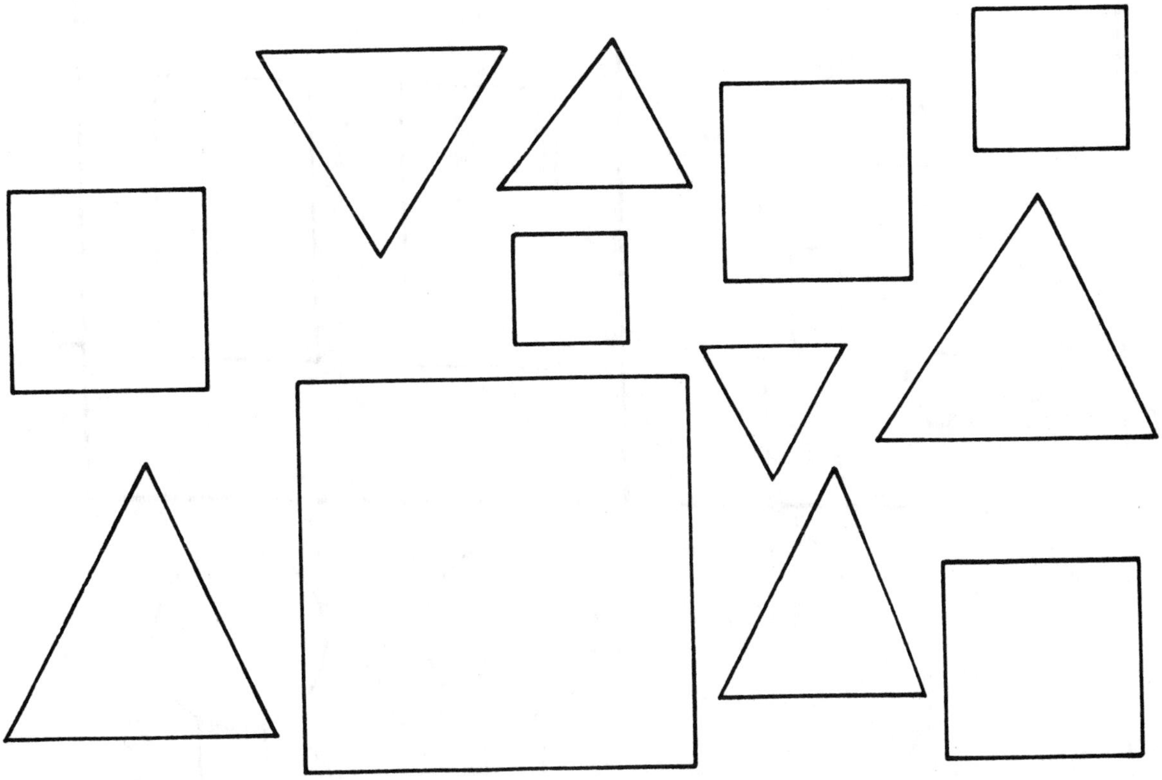

COLORS AND SHAPES

Color the squares red.
Color the circles blue.
Color the triangles yellow.
Color the rectangles green.

Skills: Shape recognition; Following directions

COLORS AND SHAPES

Color the squares red.
Color the circles blue.
Color the triangles yellow.
Color the rectangles green.

Skills: Shape recognition; Following directions

COLORS AND SHAPES

Color these things that are red.

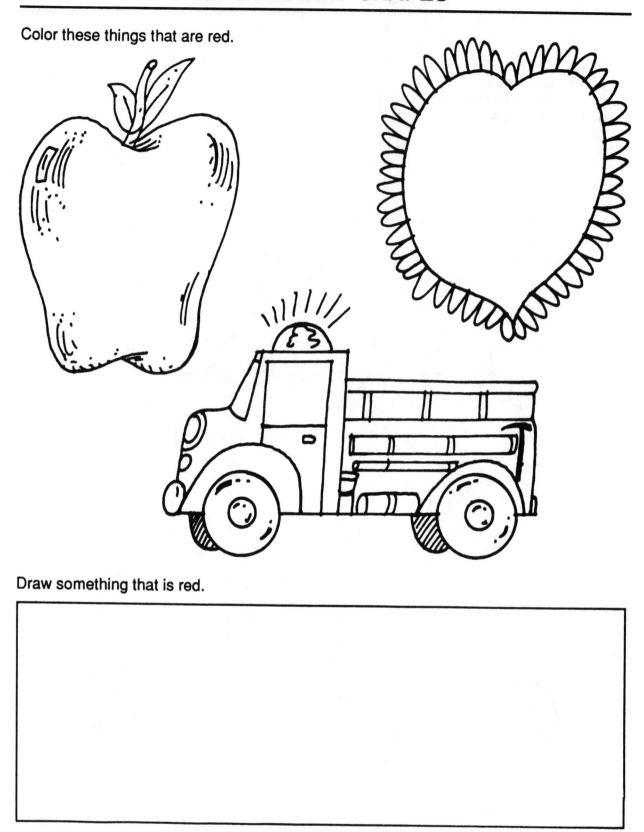

Draw something that is red.

COLORS AND SHAPES

Color these things that are purple.

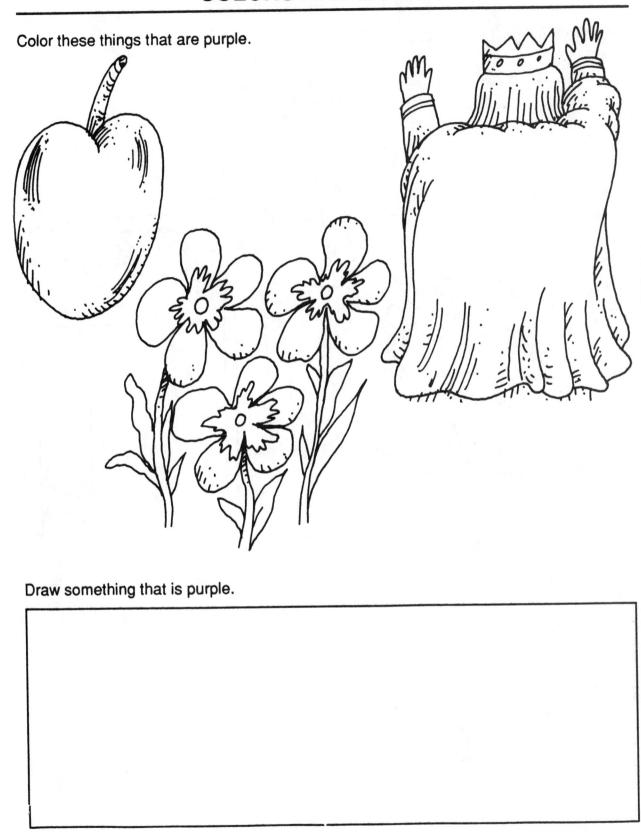

Draw something that is purple.

COLORS AND SHAPES

Color these things that are blue.

Draw something that is blue.

Skills: Distinguishing colors

COLORS AND SHAPES

Color these things that are green.

Draw something that is green.

COLORS AND SHAPES

Color these things that are yellow.

Draw something that is yellow.

Skills: Distinguishing colors

COLORS AND SHAPES

Color these things that are orange.

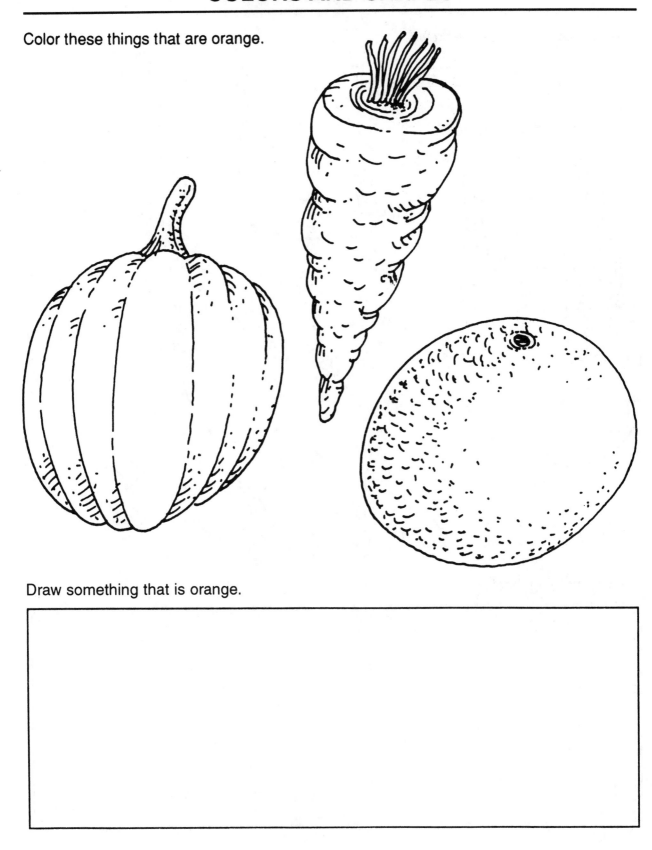

Draw something that is orange.

Skills: Distinguishing colors

COLORS AND SHAPES

Color these things that are brown.

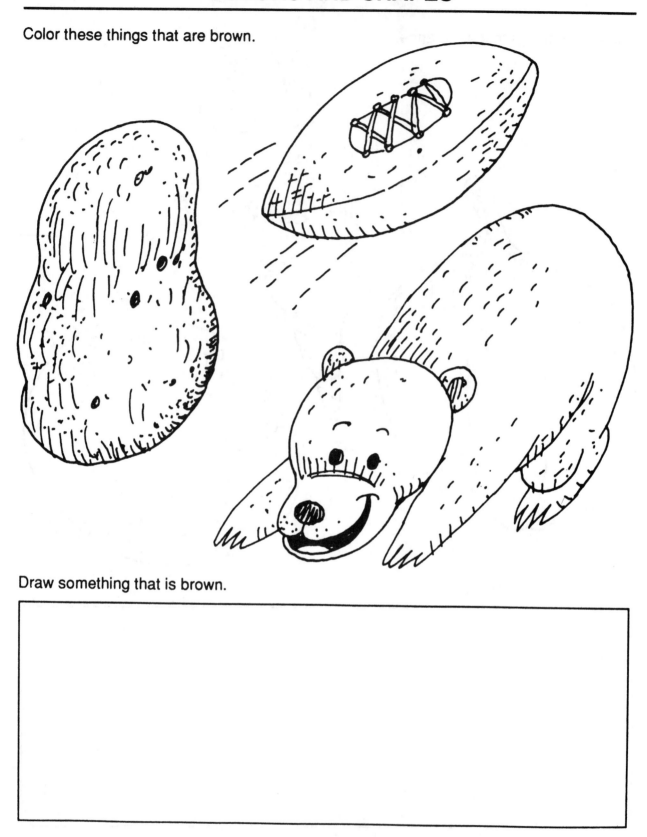

Draw something that is brown.

Skills: Distinguishing colors

COLORS AND SHAPES

Color these things that are black.

Draw something that is black.

Draw something that is black.

COLORS AND SHAPES

Look at the birds in the park.
Color each bird to match the color word.

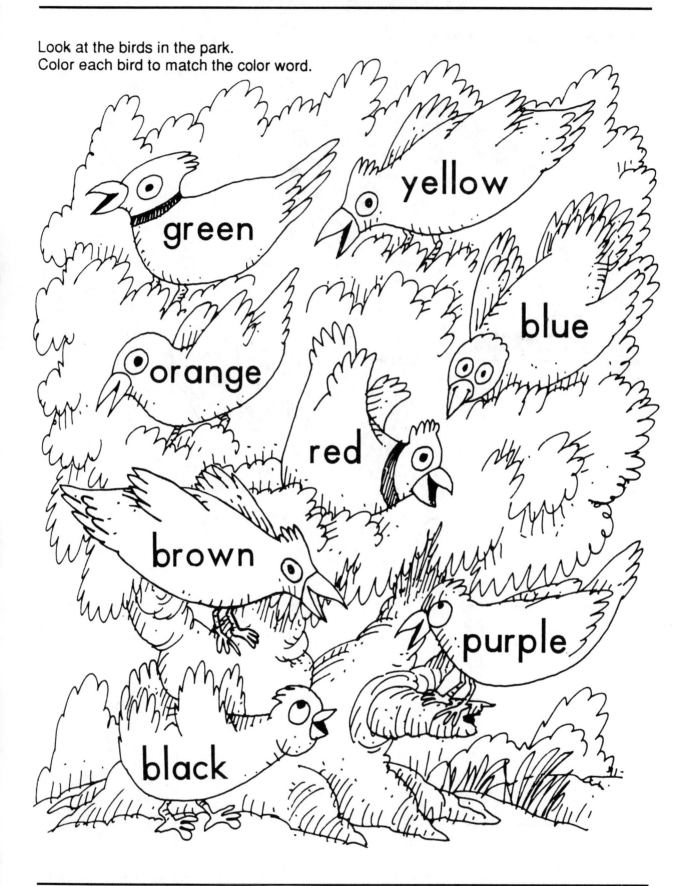

Skills: Distinguishing colors and color words

MATH READINESS SKILLS

Look at the picture in each box.
Circle the one that is on the top.
Then color the pictures.

Skills: Recognizing position (top)

MATH READINESS SKILLS

Look at the picture in each box.
Circle the one that is on the top.
Then color the pictures.

Skills: Recognizing position (top)

MATH READINESS SKILLS

Look at the picture in each box.
Circle the one that is on the bottom.
Then color the pictures.

Skills: Recognizing position (bottom)

MATH READINESS SKILLS

Look at the picture in each box.
Circle the one that is on the bottom.
Then color the pictures.

Skills: Recognizing position (bottom)

MATH READINESS SKILLS

Look at the picture in each box.
Circle the one that is in the middle.
Then color the pictures.

Skills: Recognizing position (middle)

MATH READINESS SKILLS

Look at the pictures in each box.
Circle the one that is in the middle.
Then color the pictures.

Skills: Recognizing position (middle)

MATH READINESS SKILLS

Look at the picture in each box.
Circle the one that is outside.
Then color the pictures.

Skills: Recognizing position (outside)

MATH READINESS SKILLS

Look at the picture in each box.
Circle the one that is inside.
Then color the pictures.

Skills: Recognizing position (inside)

MATH READINESS SKILLS

Look at the pattern in each row. Draw pictures to continue the pattern.
Then color the shapes.

Skills: Observing and reproducing patterns; Visual memory; Fine motor skill development

MATH READINESS SKILLS

Look at the pattern in each row. Draw a line to the picture that continues each pattern. Then color the pictures.

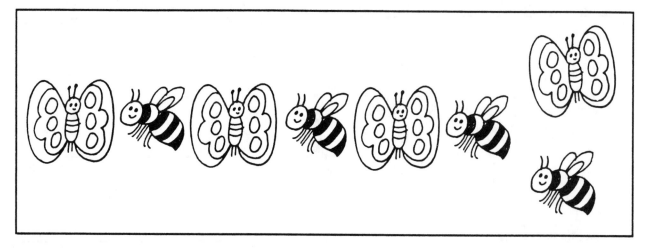

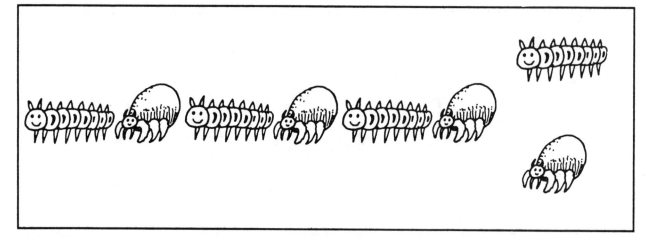

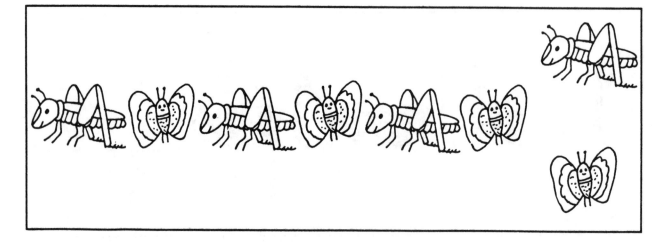

Skills: Observing and continuing patterns; Visual memory

MATH READINESS SKILLS

Look at the pattern in each row. Draw a line to the picture that continues each pattern. Then color the pictures.

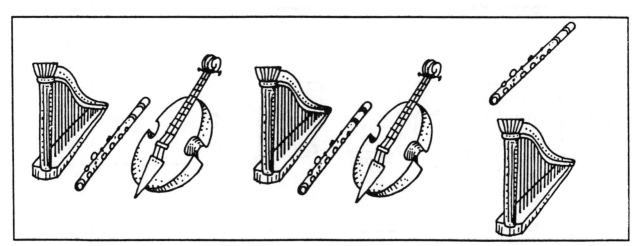

Skills: Observing and continuing patterns; Visual memory

MATH READINESS SKILLS

Look at the pattern in each row. Draw the shapes that continue the patterns. Then color the shapes.

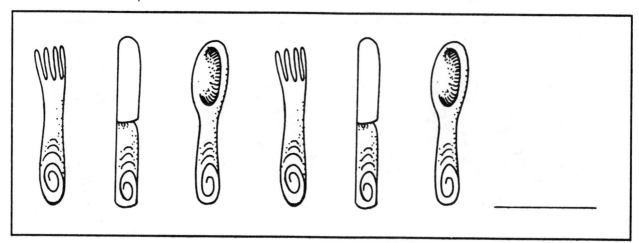

Skills: Observing and reproducing patterns; Visual memory; Fine motor skill development

MATH READINESS SKILLS

Look at these patterns. Draw a line to the picture that continues each pattern.
Then color the pictures.

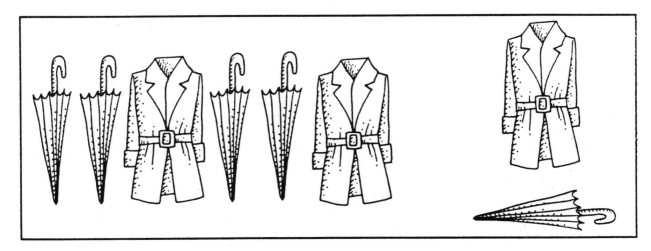

Skills: Observing and continuing patterns; Visual memory; Size discrimination

MATH READINESS SKILLS

Look at the pattern in each row. Draw the shapes that continue the patterns. Then color the shapes.

Skills: Observing and reproducing patterns; Visual memory; Fine motor skill development

MATH READINESS SKILLS

Which one is large?
Look at the pictures in each row. Circle the one that is large. Then color the pictures.

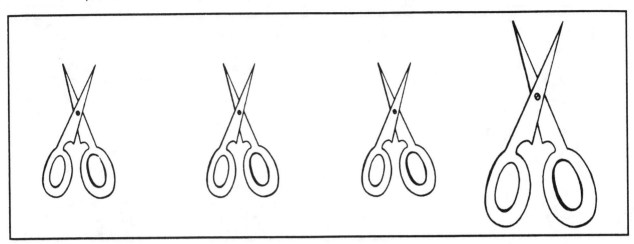

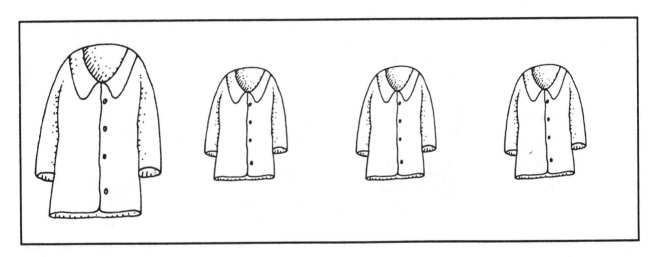

Skills: Visual discrimination; Making comparisons; Following directions

MATH READINESS SKILLS

Which one is small?
Look at the pictures in each row. Circle the one that is small. Then color the pictures.

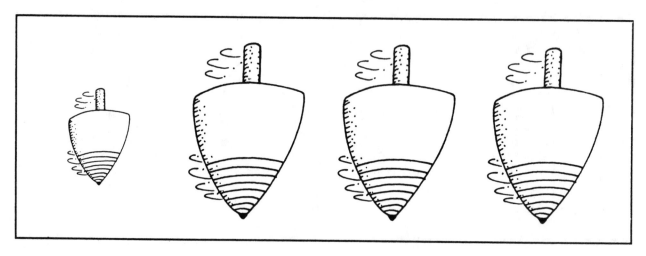

Skills: Visual discrimination; Making comparisons; Following directions

MATH READINESS SKILLS

Look at the pictures in each box. Color the small pictures green.
Color the large pictures yellow.

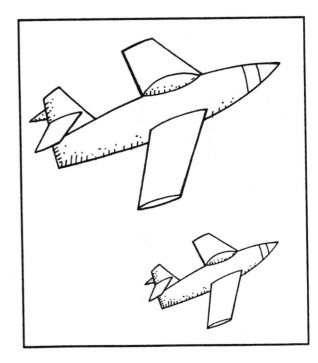

Skills: Making comparisons; Following directions

MATH READINESS SKILLS

Look at the pictures in each box. Color the small pictures red.
Color the large pictures blue.

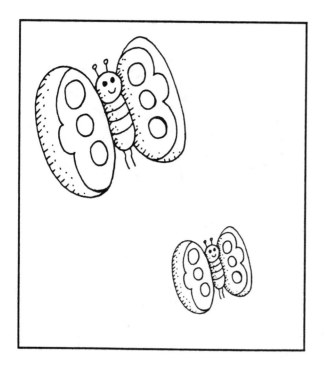

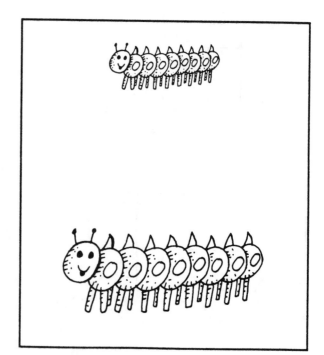

Skills: Making comparisons; Following directions

MATH READINESS SKILLS

Look at the pictures in each box.
Circle the picture of the person who is shorter.
Then color the pictures.

Skills: Making comparisons; Visual discrimination

MATH READINESS SKILLS

Look at the pictures in each box.
Circle the picture of the person who is taller.
Then color the pictures.

Skills: Making comparisons; Visual discrimination

MATH READINESS SKILLS

Which one is shorter?
Look at the pictures in each box. Circle the one that is shorter.
Then color the pictures.

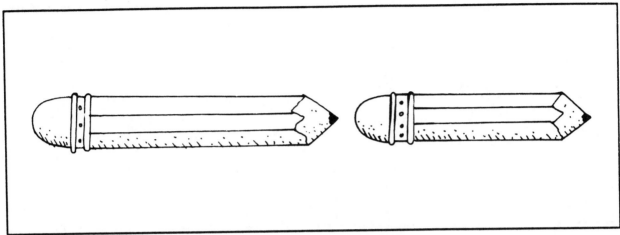

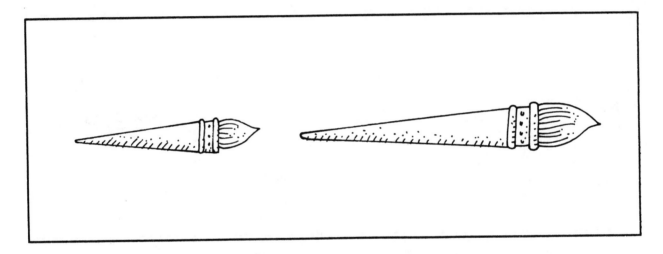

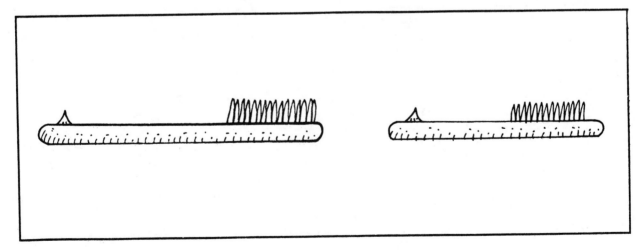

Skills: Making comparisons; Visual discrimination

MATH READINESS SKILLS

Which one is longer?
Look at the pictures in each box. Circle the one that is longer.
Then color the pictures.

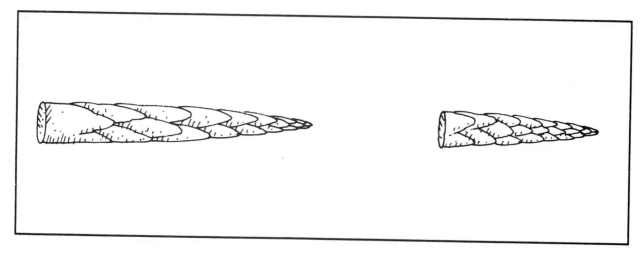

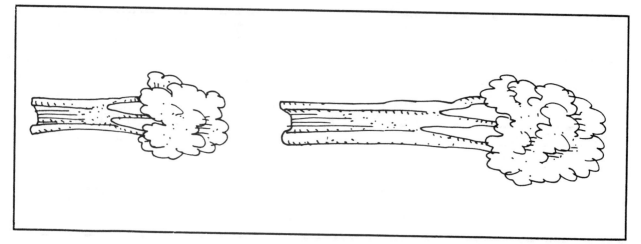

Skills: Making comparisons; Visual discrimination

MATH READINESS SKILLS

Look at the pictures in each box.
Draw lines to match the number of objects on the top to the
number of objects on the bottom. Then color the pictures.

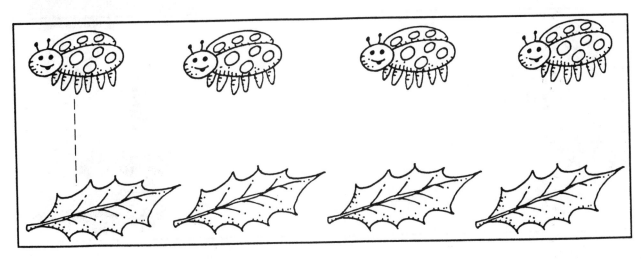

Skills: One-to-one correspondence; Association

MATH READINESS SKILLS

Look at the pictures in each box. Draw lines to match the number of objects on one side to the number of objects on the other side. Then color the pictures.

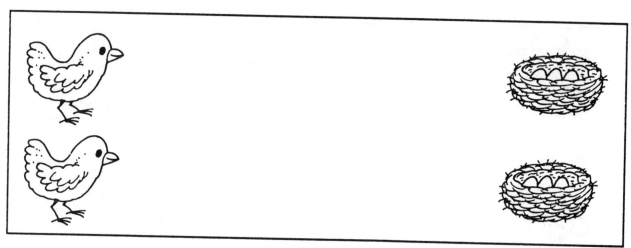

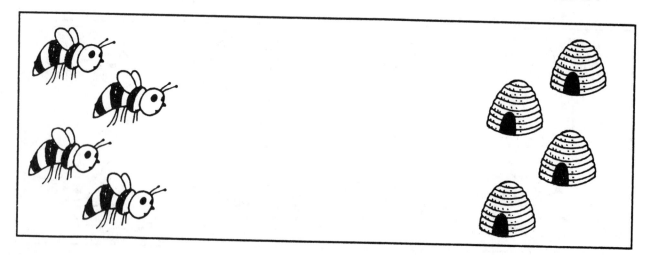

Skills: One-to-one correspondence; Association

MATH READINESS SKILLS

Look at the pictures in each box.
Draw a ball for each animal.
Then color the pictures.

Skills: One-to-one correspondence; Development of number sense

MATH READINESS SKILLS

Look at the pictures in each box.
Circle the group that shows less. Then color the pictures.

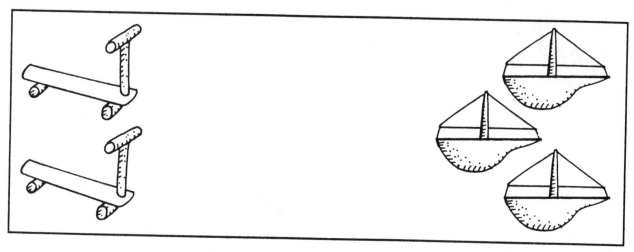

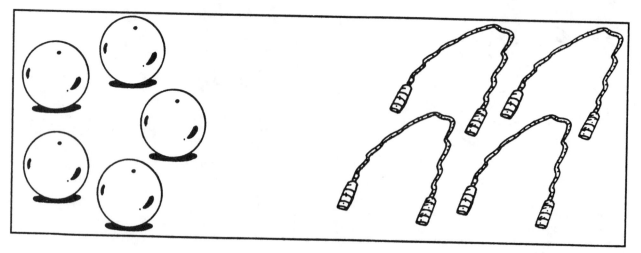

Skills: Making comparisons; Development of number sense

MATH READINESS SKILLS

Look at the pictures in each box.
Circle the group that shows more.
Then color the pictures.

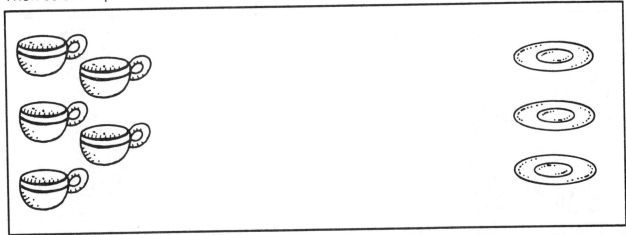

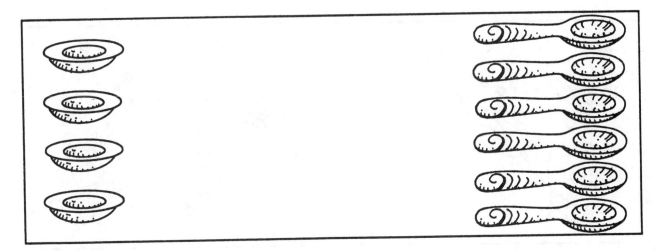

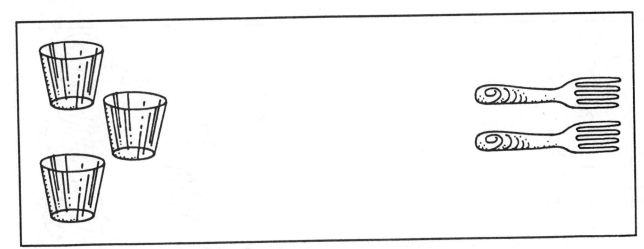

Skills: One-to-one correspondence; Classification

MATH READINESS SKILLS

Look at the pictures in each box.
Circle the group that shows more. Then color the pictures.

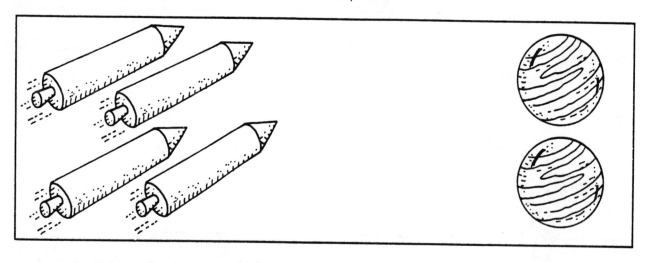

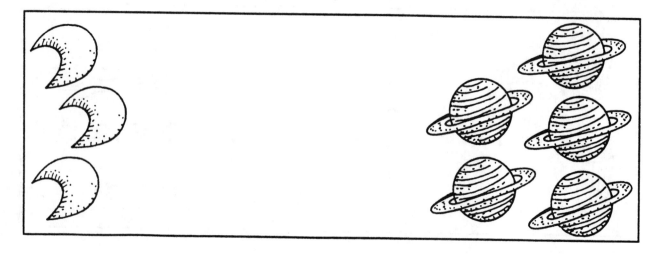

Skills: Making comparisons; Development of number sense

MATH READINESS SKILLS

Look at the pictures in each box.
Circle the group that shows less.
Then color the pictures.

Skills: One-to-one correspondence; Classification

MATH READINESS SKILLS

The turtle at the top of the page is facing right.
Circle the pictures that show turtles facing right.

Skills: Recognizing left and right; Position

MATH READINESS SKILLS

The turkey at the top of the page is facing left.
Draw a line under the pictures that show turkeys facing left.

Skills: Recognizing left and right; Position

MATH READINESS SKILLS

Look at the pictures at the top of the page.
One horse is facing right. One horse is facing left.
Circle the pictures that show animals facing right.
Draw a line under the pictures that show animals facing left.

Skills: Recognizing right and left; Position

MATH READINESS SKILLS

Look at the hands at the top of the page.
One hand is on the right. One hand is on the left.
Circle the pictures that are on the right.
Draw a line under the pictures that are on the left.

 left 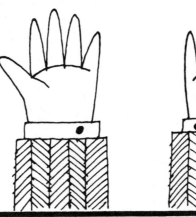 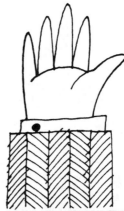 **right**

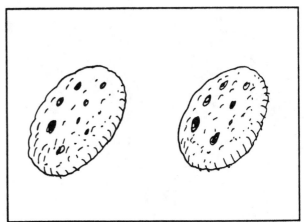

Skills: Recognizing right and left; Position

MATH READINESS SKILLS

Look at the picture in each box.
Look at the word **left** or **right** under each picture.
Circle the object that is on the **appropriate side**.

left

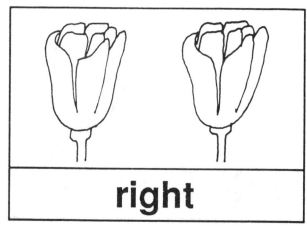

right

left

right

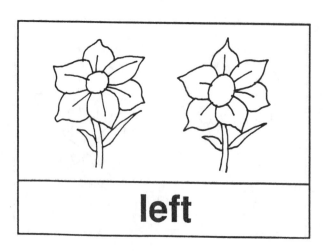

left

right

Skills: Recognizing left and right; Position

MATH READINESS SKILLS

Look at the picture in each box.
Look at the word **left** or **right** under each picture.
Circle the object that is on the appropriate side.

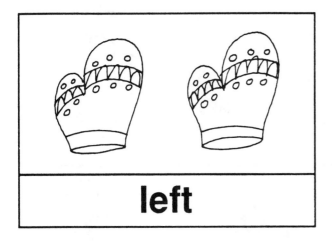

left

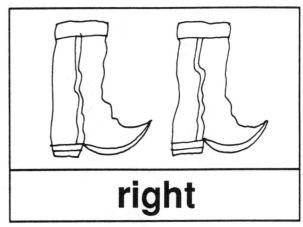

right

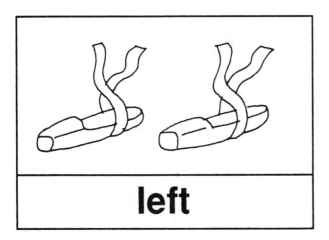

left

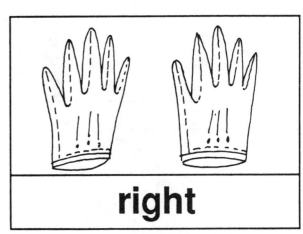

right

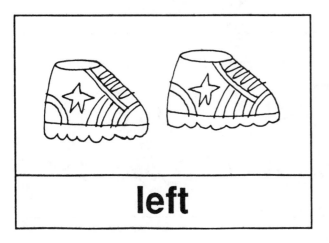

left

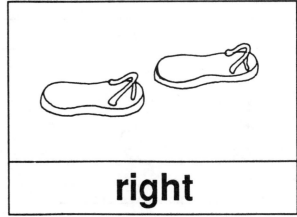

right

Skills: Recognizing left and right; Position

MATH READINESS SKILLS

Look at the pictures in each row.
Circle the picture of the animal that is first in line.
Then color the pictures.

Skills: Recognizing ordinal numbers (first); Position

MATH READINESS SKILLS

Look at the pictures in each row.
Circle the picture of the animal that is second in line.
Then color the pictures.

Skills: Recognizing ordinal numbers (second); Position

MATH READINESS SKILLS

Look at the pictures in each row.
Circle the picture of the animal that is third in line.

Skills: Recognizing ordinal numbers (third); Position

MATH READINESS SKILLS

Look at the pictures in each row.
Circle the first picture in each row.
Draw a line under the second picture in each row.
Color the third picture in each row.

Skills: Recognizing ordinal numbers (first, second, third); Position

NUMBER CONCEPTS

How many do you see?
Trace the numeral.
Then color the picture.

Skills: Recognizing a set of "1"; Forming the numeral "1"

NUMBER CONCEPTS

Look at the sets in each box.
Circle the sets that show "1".
Then color the pictures.

Skills: Identifying sets of "1"

NUMBER CONCEPTS

How many do you see?
Trace the numeral.
Then color the picture.

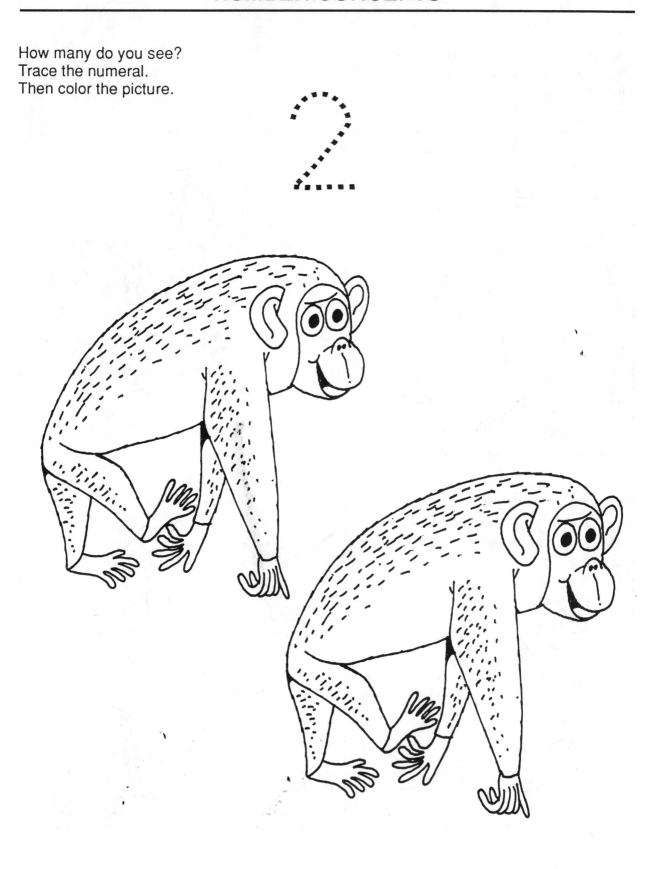

NUMBER CONCEPTS

Look at the numeral in the center of the page.
Find the sets that show 2.
Draw a line from those pictures to the numeral 2.

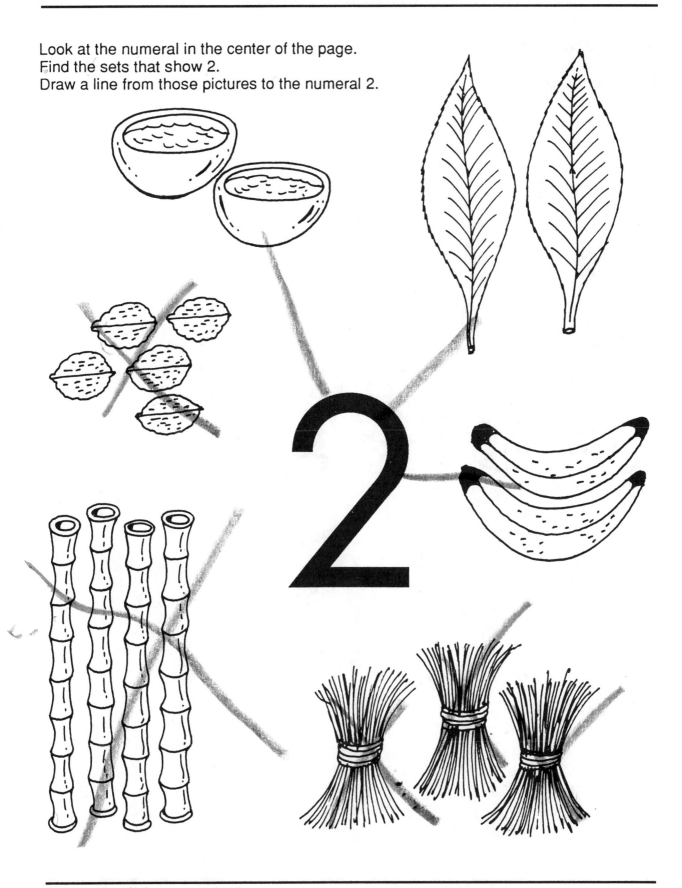

Skills: Identifying sets of "2"

How many do you see?
Trace the numeral.
Then color the picture.

Skills: Recognizing a set of "3"; Forming the numeral "3"

NUMBER CONCEPTS

Look at the pictures in each row.
Color three of each animal.

Skills: Creating sets of "3"

NUMBER CONCEPTS

How many do you see?
Trace the numeral.
Then color the picture.

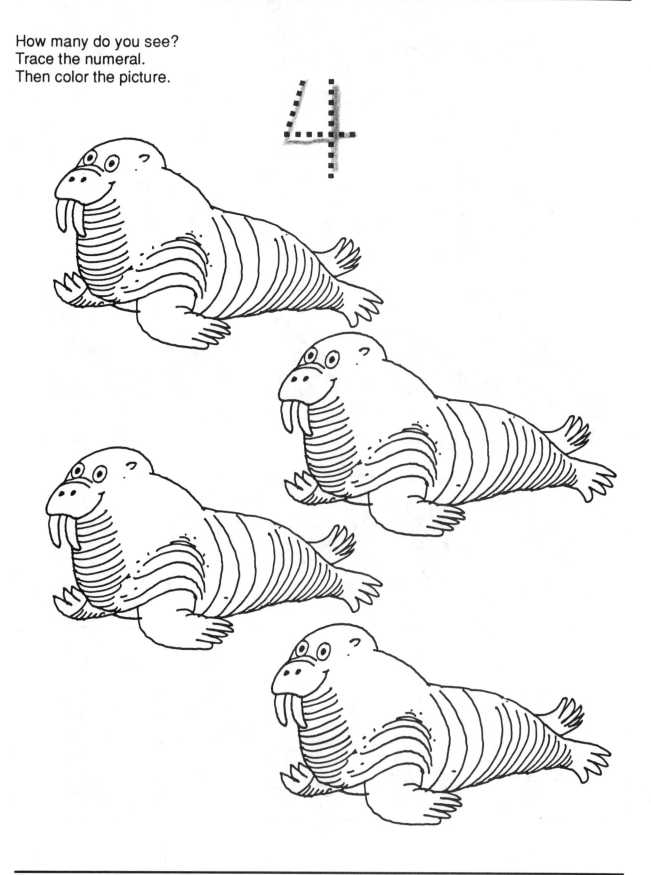

Skills: Recognizing a set of "4"; Forming the numeral "4"

NUMBER CONCEPTS

Look at the set in each box.
Circle the number that tells how many.
Then color the pictures.

3   4   5

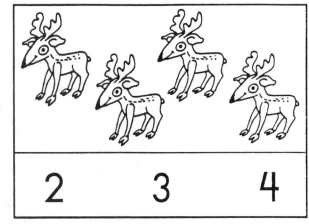

2   3   4

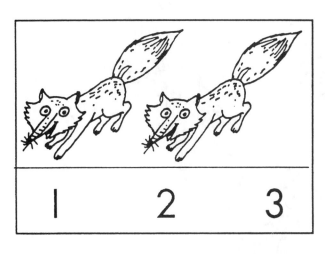

1   2   3

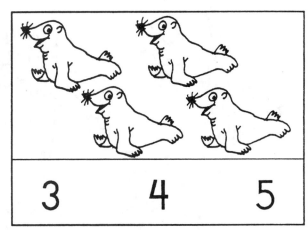

3   4   5

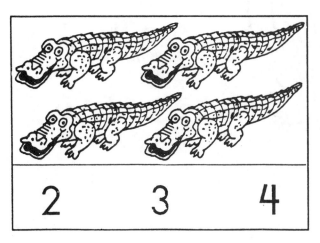

2   3   4

1   2   3

Skills: Identifying sets of "4"

NUMBER CONCEPTS

How many do you see?
Trace the numeral.
Then color the picture.

Skills: Recognizing a set of "5"; Forming the numeral "5"

NUMBER CONCEPTS

Look at the numeral at the beginning of each row.
Circle that number of animals.
Then color the pictures.

NUMBER CONCEPTS

How many do you see?
Trace the numeral.
Then color the picture.

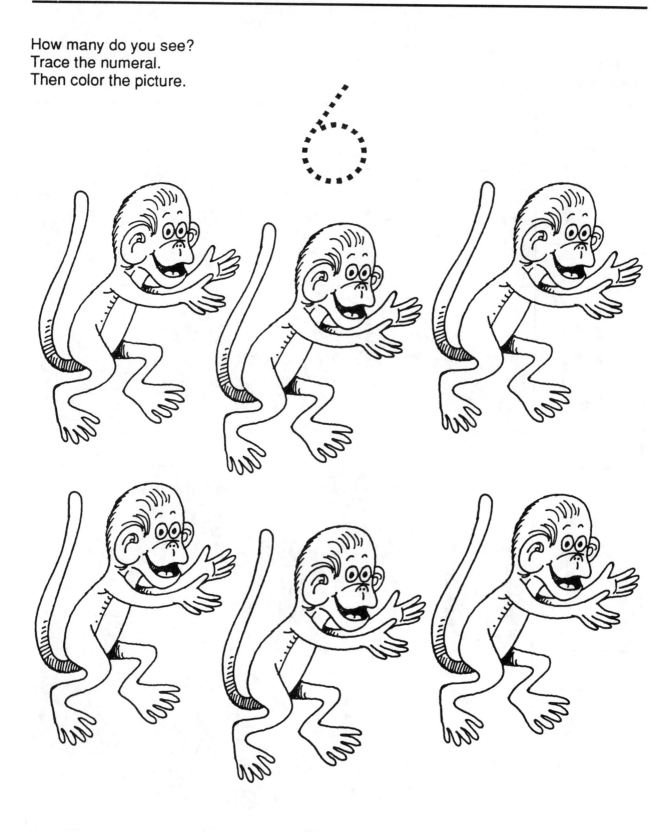

NUMBER CONCEPTS

Look at the sets in each box.
Circle the number that tells how many.
Then color the pictures.

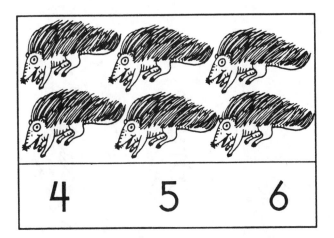

4   5   6

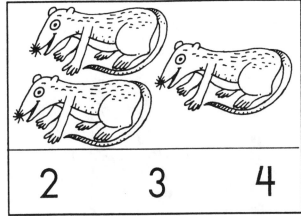

2   3   4

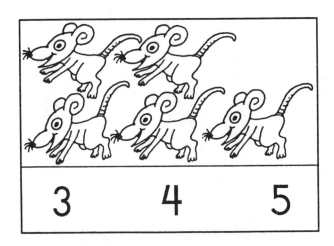

3   4   5

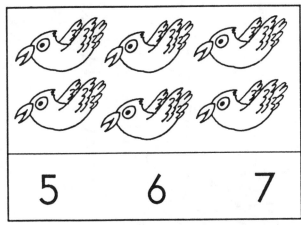

5   6   7

1   2   3

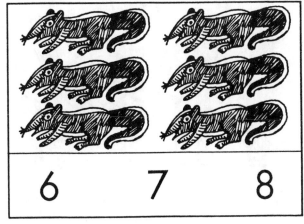

6   7   8

Skills: Identifying sets of "6"

NUMBER CONCEPTS

How many do you see?
Trace the numeral.
Then color the picture.

Skills: Recognizing a set of "7"; Forming the numeral "7"

NUMBER CONCEPTS

Look at each set.
Color the sets that show "7".

Skills: Identifying sets of "7"

NUMBER CONCEPTS

How many do you see?
Trace the numeral.
Then color the picture.

Skills: Recognizing a set of "8"; Forming the numeral "8"

NUMBER CONCEPTS

How many objects do you see in each big box?
Write the number in the small box.
Then color the sets that show "8".

Skills: Identifying sets of "8"

NUMBER CONCEPTS

How many do you see?
Trace the numeral.
Then color the picture.

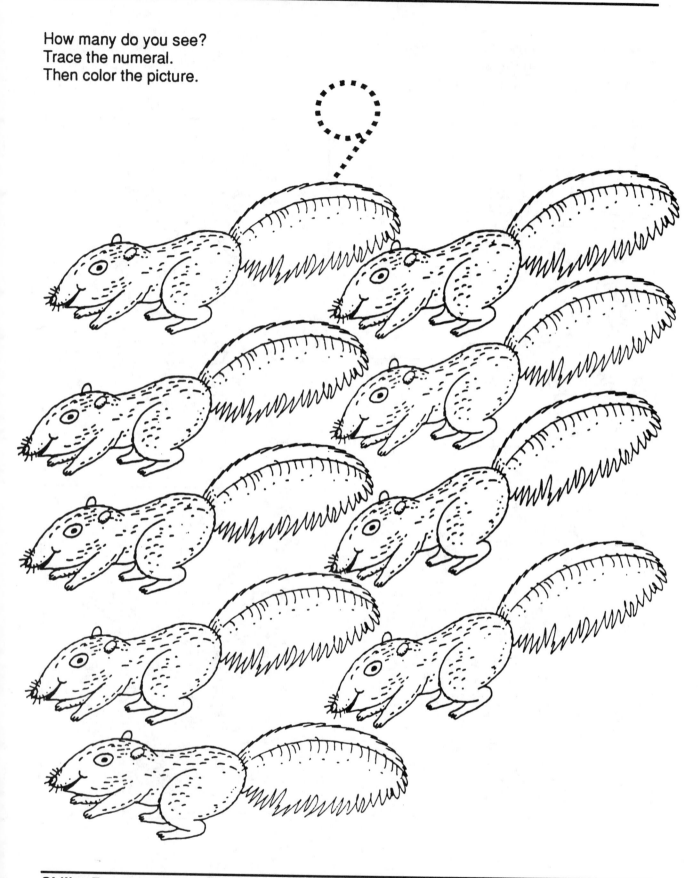

Skills: Recognizing a set of "9"; Forming the numeral "9"

NUMBER CONCEPTS

Look at each row of pictures.
Color each row to show sets of "9".

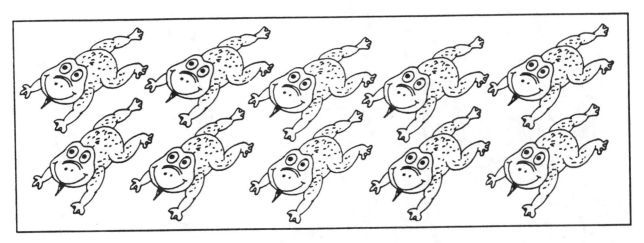

Skills: Identifying sets of "9"

NUMBER CONCEPTS

How many do you see?
Trace the numeral.
Then color the picture.

NUMBER CONCEPTS

How many objects do you see in each big box?
Write the number in the small box.
Then color the sets that show "10".

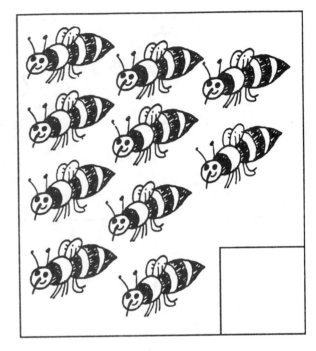

Skills: Identifying sets of "10"

NUMBER CONCEPTS

How many do you see?
Draw another set to show the same number.
Then trace and print the numeral and number word.

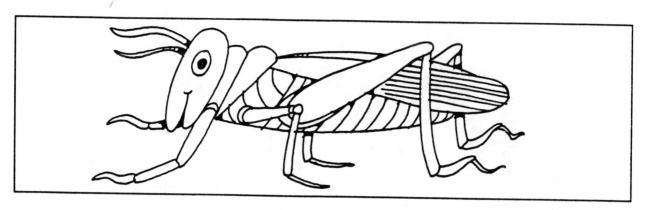

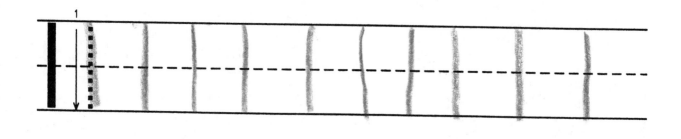

Skills: Recognizing a set of "1"; Forming the numeral "1"; Writing the number one

278

NUMBER CONCEPTS

How many do you see?
Draw another set to show the same number.
Then trace and print the numeral and number word.

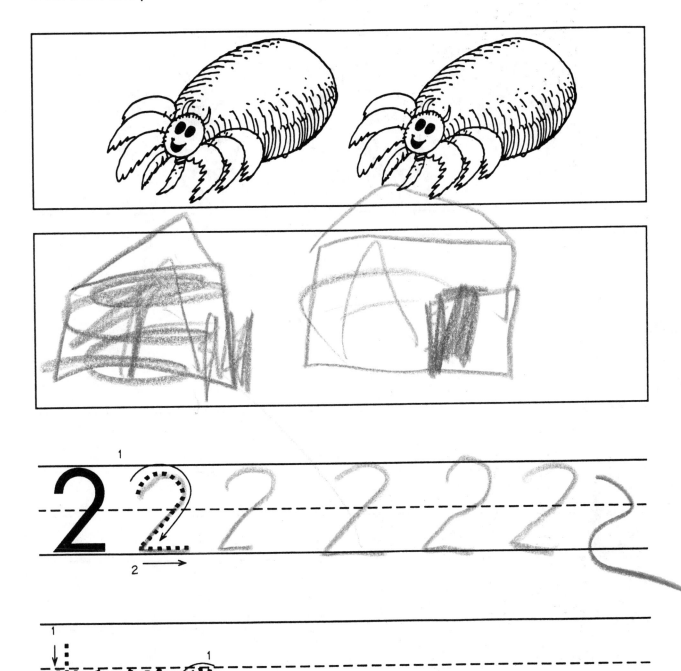

NUMBER CONCEPTS

How many do you see?
Draw another set to show the same number.
Then trace and print the numeral and number word.

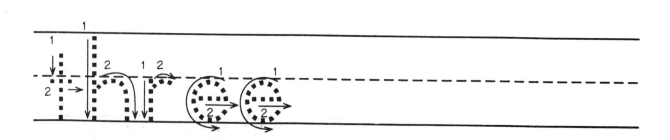

NUMBER CONCEPTS

How many do you see?
Draw another set to show the same number.
Then trace and print the numeral and number word.

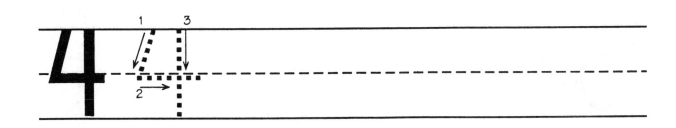

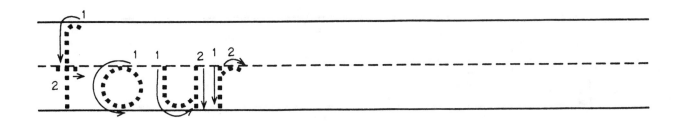

Skills: Recognizing a set of "4"; Forming the numeral "4"; Writing the number four

NUMBER CONCEPTS

How many do you see?
Draw another set to show the same number.
Then trace and print the numeral and number word.

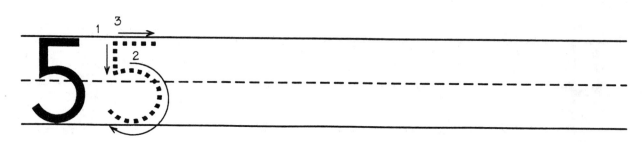

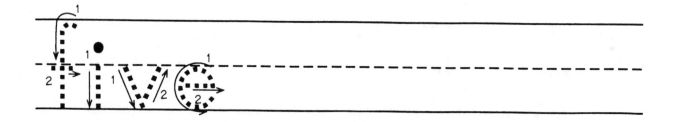

Skills: Recognizing a set of "5"; Forming the numeral "5"; Writing the number five

282

NUMBER CONCEPTS

How many do you see?
Draw another set to show the same number.
Then trace and print the numeral and number word.

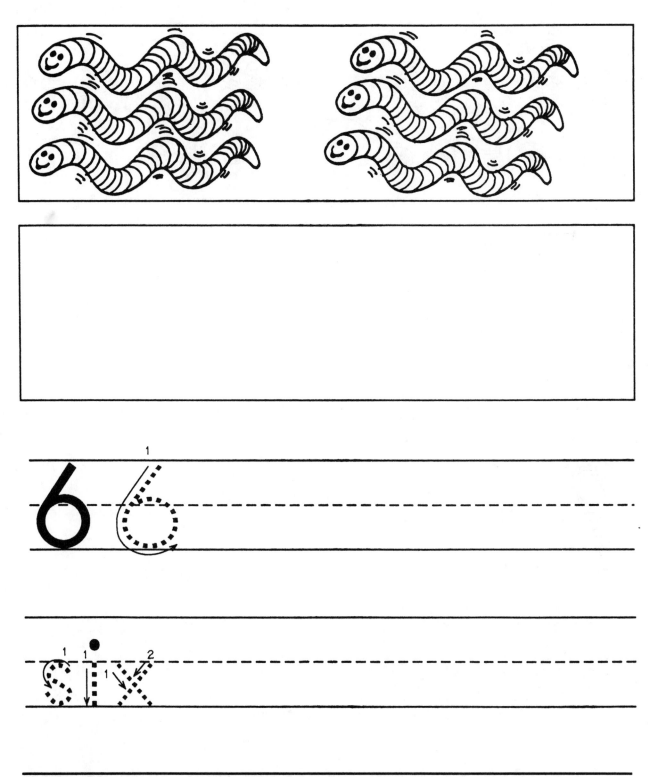

NUMBER CONCEPTS

How many do you see?
Draw another set to show the same number.
Then trace and print the numeral and number word.

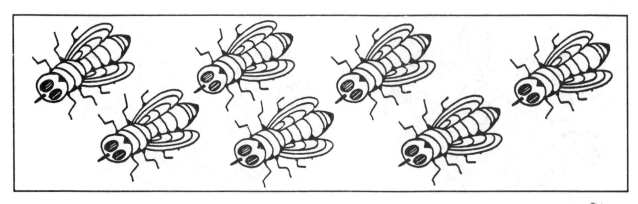

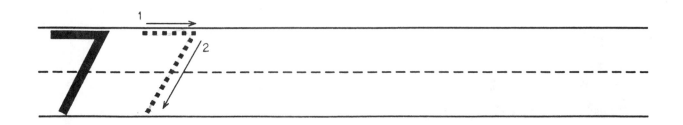

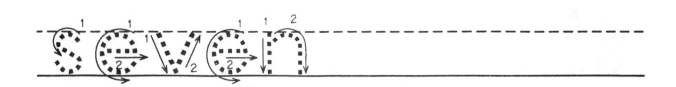

Skills: Recognizing a set of "7"; Forming the numeral "7"; Writing the number seven

NUMBER CONCEPTS

How many do you see?
Draw another set to show the same number.
Then trace and print the numeral and number word.

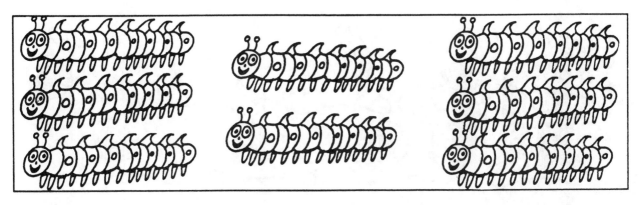

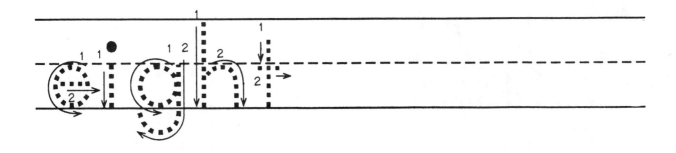

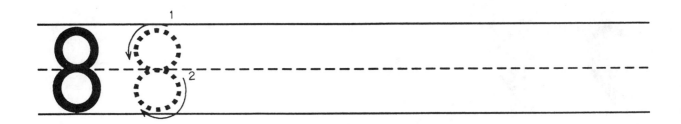

Skills: Recognizing a set of "8"; Forming the numeral "8"; Writing the number eight

NUMBER CONCEPTS

How many do you see?
Draw another set to show the same number.
Then trace and print the numeral and number word.

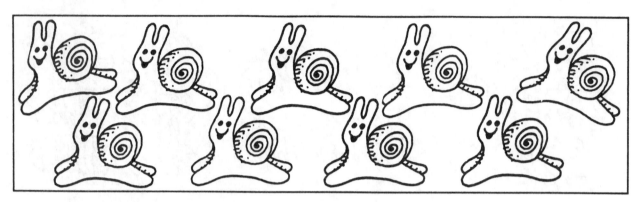

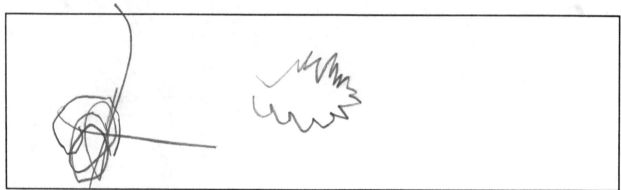

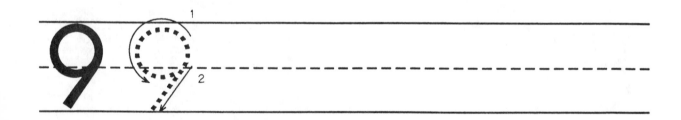

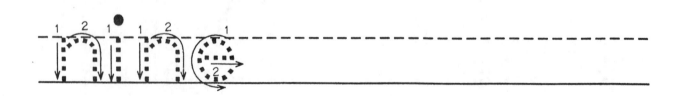

Skills: Recognizing a set of "9"; Forming the numeral "9"; Writing the number nine

286

NUMBER CONCEPTS

How many do you see?
Draw another set to show the same number.
Then trace and print the numeral and number word.

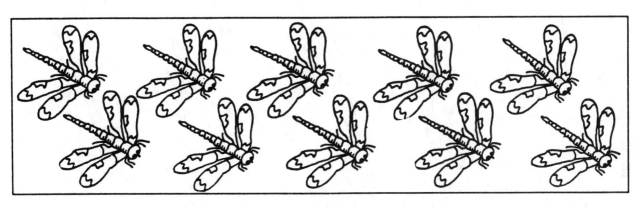

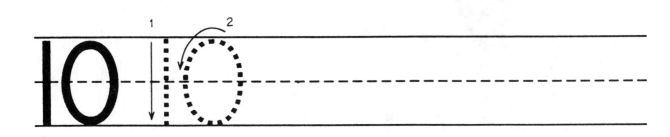

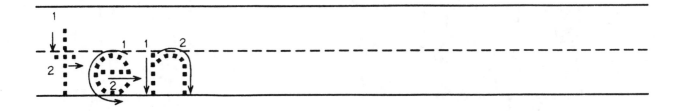

Skills: Recognizing a set of "10"; Forming the numeral "10"; Writing the number ten

NUMBER CONCEPTS

Connect the dots from 1 to 10 to find out
who lives in the hole in the tree.
Then color the picture.

Skills: Number order; Recognition of numerals

NUMBER CONCEPTS

Connect the dots from 1 to 10 to find out who is joining the picnic.

Skills: Number order; Recognition of numerals

NUMBER CONCEPTS

Connect the dots from 1 to 10 to find out who lives in the cave.

Skills: Number order; Recognition of numerals

NUMBER CONCEPTS

How many objects are in each **set**? **Draw a line** to match the sets with the same number of objects.

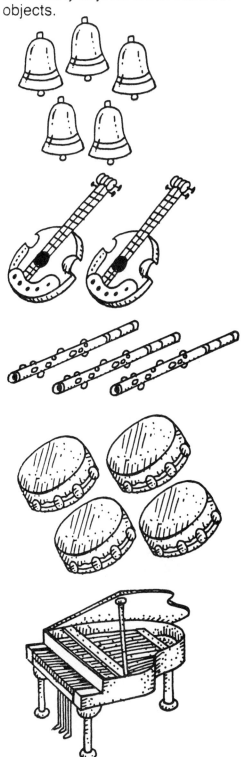
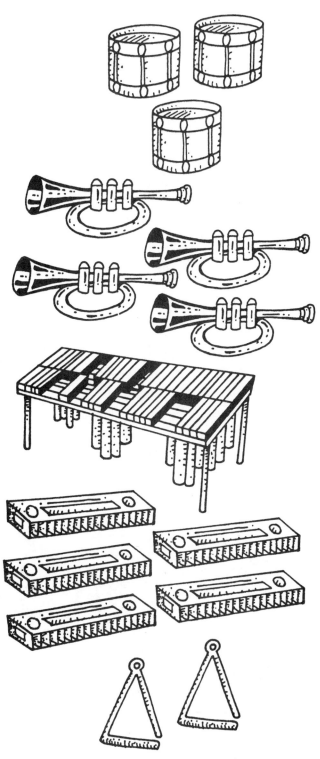

Skills: Identifying sets; Matching

NUMBER CONCEPTS

Look at the numeral on each flower pot.
Draw that many flowers in each flower pot.

Skills: Recognizing numerals; Creating sets to show an amount

NUMBER CONCEPTS

How many objects are in each set? Draw a line to match the sets with the same number of objects.

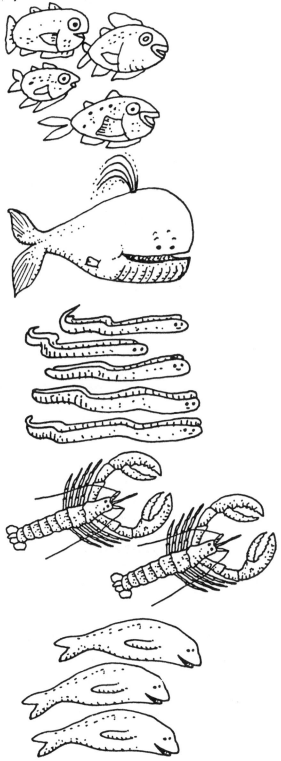
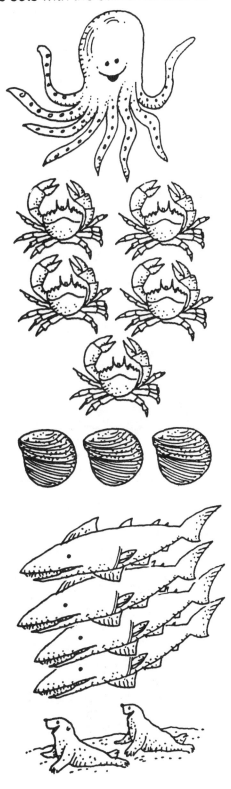

Skills: Identifying sets; Matching

NUMBER CONCEPTS

Circle the number that tells how many. Then color the pictures.

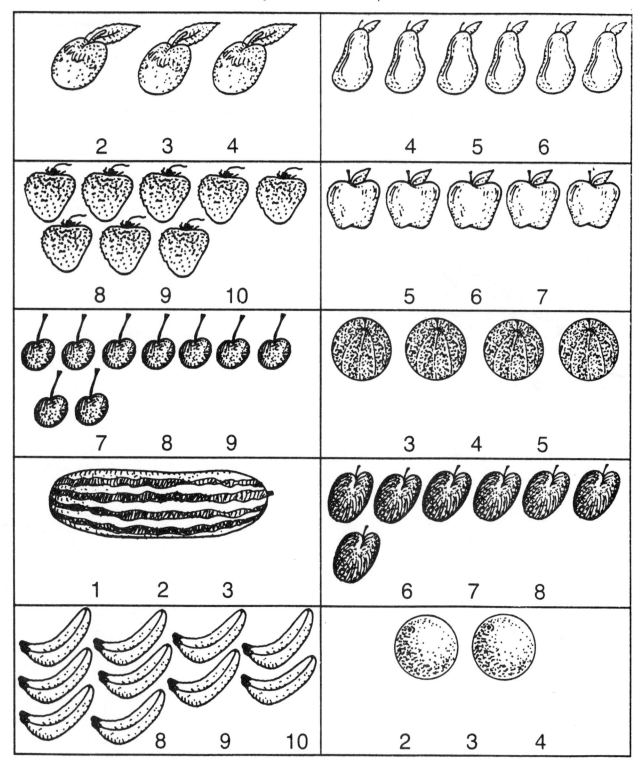